365
fun-filled
LEARNING
ACTIVITIES

you can do with your child

Disclaimer

365
fun-filled

LEARNING
ACTIVITIES
you can do with your child

....

by Mary Weaver

Adams Media Corporation
Holbrook, Massachusetts

Published by
Adams Media Corporation
260 Center Street, Holbrook, MA 02343

ISBN: 1-58062-127-9

Printed in the United States of America.

J I H G F E D C B A

Library of Congress Cataloging-in-Publication Data
Weaver, Mary.
365 learning activities you can do with your child :
for ages 3 through 7 / by Mary S. Weaver.
p.   cm.
Includes bibliographical references (p.   ).
ISBN 1-58062-127-9
1. Early childhood education—Activity programs. 2. Early childhood education—
Parent participation. I. Title. II. Title: Three hundred sixty five learning activities
you can do with your child.
LB1139.35.A37W42   1999
372.13—dc21   98-49362
CIP

Cover photo by ©Telegraph Colour Library, 1997.
Interior illustrations by Barry Littmann

This book is available at quantity discounts for bulk purchases.
For information, call 1-800-872-5627
(in Massachusetts, 781-767-8100).

Visit our home page at http://www.adamsmedia.com

Language Activities

1: Family Photos

2: Alphabet Photo Book

3: Alphabet Photo Line

4: Photo Match

5: ABC Photo Match

6: Sandpaper Letters

7: Phonics Hunt

8: Spying Phonics

9: Word Wall 1

10: Word Wall 2

11: Personal Placemats

12: Letter of the Week

13: Riddle Mania

14: Alphabet Riddles

15: Rebus Writing

16: Eat the Alphabet

17: Alphabet Book

18: Family Jobs 1

19: Family Jobs 2

20: Journals

21: Personal Address Book

22: Neighborhood Map

23: 3D Neighborhood Map

24: Fun with Food

25: Love Notes

26: News(y) Print

27: Letter Mobiles

28: Trip Souvenirs

29: The Joy of Reading

30: Wheel Sound Book

31: Become an Author!

32: Night-Time Book

33: The Play's the Thing

34: Acting It Out

35: Inventions Galore

36: Opposites

37: TV Smarts

38: Alphabet Memories

39: Supermarket Concentration

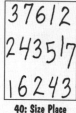

40: Size Place

41: Homemade Concentration

42: Policeman

43: Phonics Toolbox

44: It's a Puzzle!

45: Library Time

46: Beginning, Middle, and End

47: Rhyme Time

48: Rhyming Dictionary

49: Your Own Comics

50: Alphabet Antics

51: Scrambled Sentences

52: Postcard Helpers

53: Your Own VCR!

54: "I Looked out the Window"

55: It's Time to Shop!

56: A Book by Its Cover. . .

57: Shoebag Sorting

58: Peter Piper Picked a Peck . . .

59: Driver's License

60: Vowel Scavenger Hunt

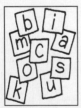
61: From "A" to "Z"

62: Pack Up!

63: Look! No Vowels!

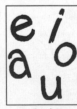
64: Vowel Sort

65: Match Up Blends

66: Spin a Sound

67: A Sentence Makes Sense

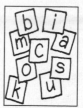
68: Magnetic Words

69: Photo Puzzle

70: Clipping Sounds

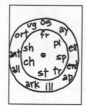
71: Blend a Word

72: Searching for Sounds

73: Lines and Curves

74: Pop-up Books

75: Shopping List

76: Charades

77: Writing to the Author

78: Sorting the Mail

79: T-shirt Design

80: Personal Tapes

81: Punctuate!

82: Book Layouts

83: Behind Your Back! Back!

84: Story Jump-starts

85: Personal Favorites

86: Love in Bloom

87: Exploring Stories

88: Reading Strategies

89: Your Own Timeline

90: Book Publishing

91: Acting Out

92: Shopping for Words

93: Story Dioramas

94: Washing with Paint

95: Music to Paint By

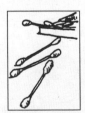

96: Tips for Painting

97: Letter Writing

98: Picture Sorts

99: Concept Building

100: Written in the Sand

101: Touchie-Feelie

102: Mind-Reading

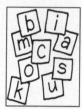
103: Before or After

104: Letter Matches

105: Rhyming Lotto

106: Alphabet Tunes

107: Spin a Letter

108: Letter Search

109: Letter Count

110: Which Is Which?

111: Alphabet Word Hunt

112: Rainy Day Reading

113: Frames for Letters

114: Step Up!

115: Following Directions

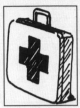

116: First Aid

117: What's That?

118: Spread the News

119: Homophones

Math Activities

120: Check Out Your Room!

121: Number Lines

122: Make a Calendar

123: Really Counting

124: Counting Hands

125: Button Number Lines

126: Juicy Counting

127: Match the Number

128: Secret Numbers

129: Roll a Number

130: Repeat!

131: Pattern Rubbings

132: Symmetry

133: Natural Symmetry

134: Fingerprints

135: Design a Pattern

136: Building Patterns

137: Pasta Patterns

138: Count and Record

139: Egg Carton Math

140: Number Books

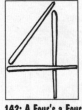

141: Surrounded by Numbers

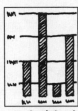

142: A Four's a Four

143: Graph Away!

144: Daily Graph

145: Tracing Shapes

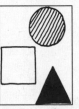

146: Shape Hunt

147: Sponge Printing

148: Geometric Art

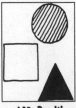

149: Bag It!

150: Sandpaper Numerals

151: The Bigger the Number . . .

152: Beginning Measurement

153: Turn Up the Volume!

154: Footloose

155: Measuring Ourselves

156: Family Measurements

157: Food Sort

158: Estimates

159: Two by Two

160: Secret Codes

161: Basic Shapes

162: Fish for Equations

163: Stop!

164: Parabolas

165: Growing Up

166: Silent Math

167: Roman Numerals

168: Shopping for Shapes

169: Keeping Track

170: Light and Heavy

171: Keeping Time

172: Beginning Time

173: Time Problems

174: Kitchen Time

175: How Long Is a Minute?

176: Number Sentence Challenge

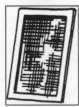
177: Weaving

178: All-Weather Weaving

179: Nature Weaving

180: Grocery Bargains

181: Counting Stamps

182: It's Laundry Time!

183: A Hundred Is . . .

184: Coin Exchange

185: Money Problems

186: Adding Coins

187: Guess My Coin!

188: Un, Deux, Trois

189: Counting by Tens

190: Bean Sticks

191: Cardboard Calculator

192: 100 Bingo

193: Bean Equations

194: Venn Diagrams

195: Catalog Shopping

196: Number Patterns

197: You've Got a Temperature!

198: Coins Only!

199: Recycling Math

200: Bank on It

201: Cutting Coupons

202: Opening a Restaurant

203: Menu Math

204: Coin Rubbings

205: Number Concentration

206: Cook with Patterns

207: Packing It Up

208: Weighing In

209: 100's Collage

210: At a Glance

211: Grouping

212: Dice Math

213: Flipping Coins

214: Odd or Even?

215: Odd/Even Sums

216: Chains of
Numbers

Science Activities

217: A Rotten Log

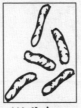
218: Mealworms

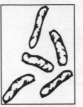
219: Mealworm Life Cycle

220: Spiders!

221: Spider Webs

222: Create a Spider

223: Minibeast Logs

224: Minibeast Riddles

225: Introducing the Slug

226: Slug Math

227: Weighing a Slug

228: Slug Races

229: Busy Bees

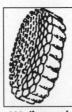
230: Honeycombs

231: Sweet as Honey

232: Miniature Gardens

233: Minibeast Terrarium

234: Balloon Creatures

235: Minibeast Prints

236: Is the Earth Flat?

237: Globe Trotting

238: Your Own Globe

239: Shadows

240: Sun Clocks

241: Water Clocks

242: Hour Glass

243: Rain and Soil

244: Sunshine

245: Frozen Mobiles

246: Leaves

247: Looking at Trees

248: Graphing Leaves

249: Leaf Match

250: Your Own Tree—Early Fall

251: Your Own Tree—Late Fall

252: Your Own Tree—Winter

253: Your Own Tree—Spring and Summer

254: Neighborhood Trees

255: Wood Sounds

256: Wood Museum

257: Visit a Lumberyard

258: Yuck!

259: Catching Some Rays

260: Color Sort

261: Nature Color Match

262: Animal Hunt

263: Visiting Animals

264: Animal Studies

265: Animal Match

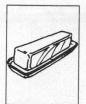
266: Animal Magnets

267: Drink Your Milk!

268: Making Butter

269: Cottage Cheese

270: Plant Life

271: Vegetable Garden

272: Carrot Top

273: Grow a Grapefruit!

274: Cold Storage

275: Sprouts

276: Sound Survey

277: Making Sounds

278: Changing Sounds

279: Water Everywhere

280: Drops of Water 1

281: Drops of Water 2

282: Water and Pipes

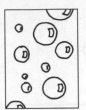

283: Bubbles!

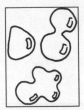

284: Bubble Shapes

285: Eye Droppers and Water

286: Hearing Test

287: Taping Sounds

288: Soda Bottle Terrarium

289: Terrariums

290: Miniature Forest

291: Woodland Creatures

292: Puddle Wonderful

293: Two of a Kind

294: Finding a Match

295: Focusing in On . . .

296: Outside Sounds

297: Country Sounds

298: Phone Me

299: Two-Way Conversation

300: Rock Collections

301: Flower Dyes

302: Buds in Bloom

303: Mystery Rainbow

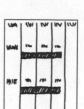

304: Weather Graph

305: Outdoor Painting

306: Make Your Own Dirt!

307: Ecosystems

308: Magnet Survey

309: Magnet Info

310: Magnet Attractions

311: Magnet Poles

312: Magnetic Power

313: Make a Magnet

314: Zooming In on Birds

315: What Makes a Bird a Bird

316: Chicken Soup

317: Toothless Birds

318: Egg Observation

319: Asking Birders

320: For the Birds

321: Preserving Leaves 1

322: Preserving Leaves 2

323: Mix It Up!

324: Putting Out Fires

325: Electricity

326: Smelling Test

327: Macie's Cookies

328: Cooking a Pumpkin

329: Fruit Salad

330: Tasting Test

331: Sewing

332: A Fixer-Upper

333: Collage a Tray

334: Hit the Stick

335: Junk Sculpture

336: Scooping Pebbles

337: Scooping Balls

338: Ladling Water

339: Spooning Escargots

340: Tweezing

341: Play Modeling Clay

342: Cornstarch Clay

343: Sponging It Up

344: Nuts and Bolts

345: Stringing Macaroni

346: Spring Cleaning

347: Shoe Shine

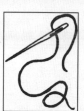

348: Threading a Needle

349: Peeling Carrots

350: Fabric Textures

351: Crayon Grating

352: Marble Painting

353: Straw Painting

354: Finger Painting

355: Pincushions

356: Pressing Flowers

357: Pressed Flower Pictures

358: Potato Prints

359: Vegetable Prints

360: Shell Out!

361: Quilting

362: Paper Mosaic

363: Toss It Around

364: Rhythm Band

365: Gymnastics

Introduction

I work in a nontraditional public school in the heart of New York City. Most of the parents have chosen our school for their children because of our commitment to a child-centered environment and in the belief that children learn at their own pace. Many of the activities in this book are extensions of learning activities found in the classroom, but also translate easily into the open-ended environment of home. All of the activities are based on the assumption that children are curious, inveterate learners who only need the opportunity, and the enthusiasm and support of their families to further their growth and development. These activities are educational as well as fun, and although all the skills to be mastered are the basis of school curriculum, using them outside the classroom only supports the idea that they count everywhere. Over time, children's repeated exposure to these basic concepts further their understanding of what must seem to them to be a very adult world. Learning doesn't stop at three o'clock!

I wish to thank my daughter Anne and the teachers of Midtown West.

Skills List

Language

Prewriting
    Alphabet Recognition
    Drawing and Painting

Writing
    Inventive Spelling
    Phonics
    Auditory Discrimination

Reading
    Visual Discrimination
    Sight Word Recognition
    Comprehension
    Critical Thinking
    Imaginative Thinking
    Language Acquisition

Math

    One-to-One Correspondence
    Sorting and Classifying
    Patterns
    Numeral Recognition
    Making Comparisons
    Counting
    Problem Solving
    Measurement
    Estimating
    Sequencing

Language Activities

Reading is language written down. A familiarity with all kinds of print—signs, ads on the cereal box, manufacturer's names on the TV or refrigerator, as well as newspapers, magazines and books—help children make the connection between speaking, writing, and reading. All beginning "writing" is drawing. The child is conveying a message each time she draws a picture. Children should always be encouraged to draw and paint and to talk about the meaning or "story" of what they have created. At the earliest level, children have shaky-fine motor skills and some activities, plus lots of time and practice, help strengthen their dexterity. When a child advances into "writing" beyond making pictures, the writing might often be lines, circles, and what educators call "marks." But to the child, this is a crucial step in the recognition of print around her.

Gradually, some alphabet letters are learned and this process eventually leads to words, and still later, sentences. At this early stage children should be encouraged to "sound out" the words they write, relying on a lot on the first sound, and eventually adding some middle and last sounds as they move on. This is an introduction to phonics called "inventive spelling" and enables the child to free herself from dependence on adults and knowing standard spelling. In the beginning, sometimes the story or message that the child writes is not what she will verbally relate when telling it. What is important is that she has reached the point where she understands the concept that writing something down conveys a message to others. This is a giant step towards literacy.

Unless otherwise specified, use lowercase letters when making letter cards, word cards, etc. Most print is in lowercase, so your child should learn to recognize lowercase letters before learning uppercase letters.

Family Photos

Go over family photographs with your child and talk about the people and events pictured. With your support, your child can help document these, especially the ones that feature her. You can take dictation, or your child can write simple labels with names and perhaps dates or maybe even a sentence or two. Arrange these photos and captions in albums and continue to work on them together over time. This activity will reinforce your child's language skills, such concepts as the passage of time, as well as the important connection of your child's position in the life of the family.

Offshoots of this activity might be an album devoted mainly to the child, sibling, a pet, vacations, or perhaps one focusing on family members that are no longer alive. This last one particularly should stimulate memories and fascinating stories from the adult involved and build a richer understanding of what "family" means.

SKILLS

✓ Sight vocabulary

✓ Inventive spelling

✓ Sequencing

Alphabet Photo Book

4 & UP

SKILLS

✓ Alphabet recognition

✓ Phonics

✓ Auditory discrimination

To create an alphabet book that has special meaning to your child, find photographs of familiar objects (or scenes) that begin with a particular letter of the alphabet. You write or have the child copy and write the letter under the photo. Before you begin this project, talk to your child about making such a book. Wherever you are, point out some items and name their beginning letter and sound. Depending on the child's developmental level, you could do a lot of the finding, and your child could find just a letter, but definitely be aware of the letter-and sound-correspondence your child does have, and help him "find" certain items that you know are easy for him.

The simplest way to begin this activity is to go about the house finding items that begin with a particular letter and photographing them. The most challenging would be to start with "a" and proceed to "z." Alternatives might be an "inside the house" or an "outside the house" format or limiting the search to one room.

2

Alphabet Photo Line

Instead of making an alphabet book using photos as illustrations, you could make an alphabet line with photos on long strips of construction paper that you staple together. You could either write the letter and then staple an appropriate photo next to it or staple the photo underneath the letter it represents. This long line of letters and pictures can be hung around the walls of your child's room as a border or along the length of a hallway. Keep in mind that the photos need to be seen, so don't hang the photo line too high.

SKILLS

✓ Alphabet recognition

✓ Phonics

✓ Auditory discrimination

Photo Match

SKILL

✓ **Visual discrimination**

Photograph familiar objects (such as a teddy bear, rug, or a nearby building) in your environment and get two copies of each photo developed. Mount each on a piece of construction paper or cardboard, cover with clear contact paper, and cut them out. Then play "Concentration" with them by shuffling them or laying them face-down on a table or floor and taking turns turning over two at a time. The object is to find a match. This game reinforces the memory of where the cards are placed, so as the game goes on your child can make an "educated" guess as to the whereabouts of certain pictures.

ABC Photo Match

Photographs connected to your child's own life make any activity more interesting and memorable. You can make an alphabet matching game using photos that represent different letters. Have two of the same photos for a particular letter, or, to make the game more challenging, use two different photos for a letter. For example: a piano and a pet for "p." Mount them on index cards and write the beginning sound/letter at the bottom. You needn't cover every letter of the alphabet, but when you have at least twenty cards you can turn them face-down in rows on a table and play "Concentration" with them.

SKILLS

✓ **Alphabet recognition**

✓ **Phonics**

✓ **Auditory discrimination**

5

SKILL

✓ Alphabet
recognition

Sandpaper Letters

To build alphabet recognition buy some sandpaper at the hardware store and some alphabet stencils. Outline each letter on a piece of sandpaper and then cut it out. Mount each letter on a piece of sturdy cardboard. These letters are appealingly tactile to your child. Encourage her to feel the letters, first by just exploring them with you and then by watching you demonstrate with your finger the correct formation of the letter. You might guide your child's finger around each letter as you say its name.

You could make an uppercase and a lowercase sandpaper alphabet and then play a matching "Concentration" game or simply match the uppercase and lowercase letters with your child.

Phonics Hunt

Have an alphabet phonics hunt with your child. Buy a clipboard or make your own with a piece of heavy cardboard and a clip or large paperclip. On it put a piece of paper folded into two or more columns. Top each column with a letter. (Use only consonants, starting with the most familiar, such as "m," "s," or "b." Vowels are much less easy to identify, although "A: for apple" is an exception.) Your child and you can search around the house for objects beginning with each letter and you can write the word down. For a young child, the object is not the writing but the ability to identify the beginning sound associated with the letter.

SKILLS

✓ Phonics

✓ Auditory discrimination

Spying Phonics

SKILLS

✓ Phonics

✓ Auditory discrimination

This is a good activity for riding in a car, but you can do it on a walk outside or just around the house if you carry a clipboard with you. In a way, it's a version of "I Spy," but the idea is to hunt for objects that begin with a certain letter. Each time your child spies an object beginning with "m," for example, he then writes down the letter "m" on his clipboard. Then at the end of the search (which might go on for days, if your child likes this game), you can count how many examples of "m" he's found.

If your child wants you to write down the name of the actual object, this activity could become a letter/word search and could be used to reinforce or introduce certain sight words. But don't push. At its simplest, this activity further extends the idea that letters and words are all around us.

Word Wall 1

For children at any stage of beginning reading, it might be useful to create a "word wall" in a convenient place. The front of the refrigerator could be used for magnetic letters, but a spot in your child's room might also make sense. If your child is just beginning to recognize her own name, the word "wall" could begin with familiar objects and family names, such as "Mom" and "Dad." Figure out how you want to do this. The easiest way is simply to write the word on a piece of construction paper and use masking tape to fix it on the wall. Maybe your child would like to illustrate the words as well.

5 & UP

SKILL

✓ **Sight word recognition**

9

playing with dolls

SKILL

✓ Sight word
   recognition

Word Wall 2

For older children, the words in your word wall could coincide with simple books being read at home or at school and could feature words, particularly nouns, from them. High-frequency words, such as "the," "in," "it," or "and," might be added at some point, but only when they figure in your child's reading vocabulary.

Obviously, a word wall can be a movable and changeable feast. As your child grows, it might include homework words or sticky ones that need review. The point, though, is to make it colorful and personal, and therefore fun, as well as useful.

Personal Placemats

To help reinforce your child's written vocabulary of family names, it's a fun idea to make individual place mats for each member of the family. Cut out the desired size of construction paper (use a light color, so the drawing and writing show up) and have your child write each person's name (with or without help) and then draw a picture, possibly of that person or simply some decorative art. Then cover each side of the paper with clear contact paper, and voilà—you have a useful and personalized addition to your meals!

SKILL

✓ Sight word recognition

Letter of the Week

Although it has a ring of school about it, having a letter of the week or even the month can be a fun at-home activity if it's kept free and easy. At an early stage, the refrigerator and magnetic letters might be an appropriate place to start. Select an obvious letter, possibly the one beginning your child's name. Then refer to it as the "letter of the week" and continue to find words beginning with that letter throughout the week. The sound of the letter should also be emphasized. The letter of the week might reflect letters and sounds the child is working on in school. Of course, you could include more than one letter at a time, but for a young child just getting started, one at a time is less complicated. Keep it easygoing and encourage contributions from everyone as long as the child or children you have in mind can benefit. The letter itself, the sound it makes, and the words build a foundation for reading skills in an nonpressured way.

Riddle Mania

Children love riddles. You and your child can make a riddle book, with one page giving the clues and the next the answer. Or you can make a riddle game, helping your child figure out clues and writing them on one side of a card and putting the illustration or answer on the other side. Coming up with clues about something can be a challenge. Try to follow a certain format at first, such as "Is it a food?" ". . . An animal?" ". . . A person?" "What color is it?" "Is it hard?" "Is it soft?" "Is it hot?" "Is it cold? The clues will get more sophisticated as the child's experience grows. Of course, this is a good game to play in the car without cards when the techniques become familiar.

5 & UP

SKILLS

✓ Imaginative thinking

✓ Critical thinking

Alphabet Riddles

SKILLS

✓ Alphabet
   recognition

✓ Phonics

✓ Auditory
   discrimination

✓ Critical thinking

Another version of a riddle book could be to restrict the riddle answer to a certain letter and having only one clue. For example, "It begins with the letter 's' and it's a small red fruit." Or, "It's a word for 'not happy.'" For a book or card game, help your child determine what the object is and then come up with three or four clues. For example: (1) "I am a fruit," (2) "I am yellow," (3) "I am sour." Your children will be excited by the game even when the riddles are familiar.

Rebus Writing

An enjoyable activity is to do rebus writing. Since it is just another form of writing, it can be used for fun in making books, writing notes to each other, and rewriting poems or familiar nursery rhymes. A rebus is a picture instead of a word, and a good way to begin is to write some of the words of a nursery rhyme and substitute a picture for other words. For example for "Jack and Jill" have your child draw pictures of Jack and Jill as well as the pail, the hill, and any other words that can be represented by a picture.

Choose a well-known rhyme to do together. This activity might work well if you're making a card to send to someone with more than "I love you." Instead, a nursery rhyme, short poem, or message in rebus form could be the greeting inside.

5 & UP

SKILL

✓ Imaginative thinking

15

Eat the Alphabet

SKILLS

✓ Alphabet recognition

✓ Sight word recognition

Alphabet cereal is just asking to be used for alphabet-sorting activities! Why not make some family name cards and pour the cereal on a tray so your child can match up the letters in the names? Ask her to name the letter she's looking for and then when she finds it, to place it underneath the corresponding letter on the card. Of course, this could work for some basic sight words as well. You might also try putting out an alphabet line or alphabet cards and asking your child to place a cereal letter on the appropriate match. Then, she can eat them!

Alphabet Book

You and your child might enjoy making an alphabet book. All of the books you make together not only function as a learning activity of the moment, but also can serve as a resource in future activities and for homework. To make a personal alphabet book, fold seven sheets of paper in half. The front is the cover and your child can write or copy the words "My Alphabet Book" or decorate it in any colorful way. Put the date on it for future reference. When you flip up this cover page, the upper half is for the letter "a" and the bottom for "b." You can write the letters, both uppercase and lowercase on a line that crosses the page, and if your child is ready, she can continue the letters across. Then the idea is to draw a picture that represents the particular letters. For embellishment, you can "label" or write the word for the illustration. A larger version of this book might include more than one picture for each page. It's up the two of you—maybe cutting out magazine pictures would be more appealing than drawing, or maybe the book could include both.

Family Jobs 1

Every family, regardless of its size, needs to think of appropriate responsibilities for its members. It can be helpful to assign certain tasks for children to encourage both their need for independence within the family and to offer the simple satisfaction that anyone of any age feels when a job is accomplished. To organize a child's chores make a colorful homemade job chart. If your child is already in preschool or "regular" school, the chart might replicate a similar one at school. Making a job chart can go in many different directions. You could simply have an envelope with each child's name on it and cards with various illustrated jobs inside and paperclip the "Job of the Week" on the outside. Or, of course, you can make a monthly chart with the days of each week and the specific jobs to be checked off in each space. For a young child, the illustration is the message, so make sure each job has an appropriate picture accompanying it.

Family Jobs 2

4 & UP

Make an envelope chart by either gluing envelopes onto sturdy construction paper or sewing or gluing felt or other fabric "envelopes." On each pocket is the name and illustration of the "job" and in the pocket is a card with the child's name showing above the edge. For a permanent chart, put Velcro on the backs of the illustrated job and on the envelopes as the tasks might change over time. A monthly format is a good one, with jobs for each child changing each month. It's up to you and your child to determine the range of chores (taking out the garbage, feeding the cat, putting the toys away) and the number of chores a week—one or two should suffice. This should inspire some sort of satisfaction— not dread!

SKILLS

✓ Sight word recognition

✓ Visual discrimination

Journals

Remember keeping a diary or journal as a teenager? Young children can also gain satisfaction from keeping a simple chronicle of their days. Perhaps just a picture can capture an activity or an inspiration of the moment. In general, it's a good idea for each page to be dated, either by you or by your child. This underlines the passage of time. Again, depending on your child's literacy level, a sentence about the specific activity illustrated or a word might be valuable and serve as a very personal way to encourage acquisition of sight vocabulary. Of course, another good reason for dating each entry is to reinforce number sense and the months of the year. From the beginning, support the idea that a journal is a record to be kept (and possibly to be kept secret, if there are siblings). The old standby black-and-white notebook is a sturdy choice (your child can collage the cover), but you can buy a fancy blank page version in a stationary store as well.

Personal Address Book

One of the first safety practices that many parents teach their school-age child is to help them memorize their address and phone numbers. This is often done long before a child can read or even write such information. When your child is interested in print, however, you can make a family/friend address book. The actual writing can be done entirely by an adult, and the child can then draw a portrait of the particular person. Or, of course, the child can write or copy all or part of the address and phone number. Alphabetizing things is a big leap for young children, but simple rote learning of the alphabet is easier and can be fostered by such an activity. In making an address book, you could write the alphabet down, leaving space for names. You yourself will probably be responsible for supplying most of the names. Keep it focused on a core list of family and friends—this is for your child, not you. Eventually, it can become a useful tool for addressing cards and letters and making phone calls.

5 & UP

SKILLS

✓ Alphabet recognition

✓ Sight word recognition

✓ Drawing

21

SKILLS

✓ Critical thinking

✓ Drawing

✓ Estimating

✓ Measurement

Neighborhood Map

A simple map could be a useful tool in explaining the neighborhood or learning routes to and from important places such as school, grandparents' house, or familiar stores. Don't get too complicated and feel you need to include every building and landmark. Instead, work on general skills, like direction and distance and recognition of what your child knows about his environment. A good way to begin is to take a brief walk or to drive and talk about what you notice, such as the huge tree in front of the corner house, the firehouse on the next block, or the two streets you need to cross to get to the supermarket. Then, at home, you both can write or quickly draw what you remember for reference. Then lay out a simple grid on large paper—a square block, one or two streets, or maybe the route to school. If the grid encompasses a fairly large area, omit a lot of detail. If you draw the streets, your child can trace over them, but help your child concentrate on particular images that he can then draw.

22

3D Neighborhood Map

Creating a map of your neighborhood can help your child both to develop her observational skills and to begin to comprehend spatial ones. Walk around your neighborhood with your child and take along a clipboard. Notice things together, such as the kinds of buildings on your street, the trees, and maybe how much traffic there is. Write down your child's descriptions, and when you get home, help her make a simple rectangle on a large piece of paper. Then work together to draw the buildings and other features. It doesn't have to be accurate— what you're putting down on paper is just a general view.

For a 3D effect on your map, use playdough or plasticine to replicate houses, plants, or people. For trees, you can collect bits of twigs, small leaves, and seeds and glue them onto the drawings. Lego constructions might also be useful for buildings, cars, or even people and will help animate the map. Little by little, more details can be added as your child notices them. The map can become the backdrop for all kinds of imaginative play.

23

Fun with Food

It's important to have lots of magazines and printed materials to use for learning activities at home. On a rainy afternoon, see if your child would like to make a collage of food from magazines. This can be as simple as a "food collage," but it could also be a collection of favorite foods on one paper and not-so-favorite ones on another. Cutting skills vary, particularly at different ages. Keep in mind that for a young child, a lot of cutting is impossible, and one way to get around this is for your child to rip out the pictures, which you can cut and they can glue. Or, you can rip them out in advance and let the child choose the pictures, which you can hold while the child cuts. Obviously, the cutting will be roughly defined but sorting pictures into groups or just choosing photos of food develops skills in visual discrimination, and the cutting and pasting are good practice in small motor skills. And the end result is art.

Love Notes

When your child is beginning to read, write some simple notes to him, using mostly words he knows. You might put a note on his pillow before he goes to bed, saying, "I will read you a book." You can add the name of a familiar book. On a weekend morning, write a breakfast note saying one special thing that will happen that day, such as "We will make a cake." Or, how about a note in his book bag? "We can go to the park with Julie after school." Sometimes a note stuck in your child's coat pocket is just the right kind of message for him during the day away at school. How about, "I Love You?"

5 & UP

SKILL

✓ Sight word recognition

News(y) Print

SKILLS

✓ **Alphabet recognition**

✓ **Sight word recognition**

✓ **Manual dexterity**

At the earliest level of alphabet and print recognition, just the understanding that letters have to do with words and with reading can draw a young child to seek out print in the environment and to recognize certain letters and later on, words. Newspapers and magazines can be excellent sources of easy-to-read print, as headlines and ads use extra-large letters that stand out and are easy to spot by children. You can use these printed letters or words in all sorts of activities. You could simply make an alphabet line, or your child could cut out and paste letters for her name and those of the family (copying the written names you provide). A container of letters or useful words ("baseball," "alien," "fantastic," "Hercules," etc.) can be kept to be used to occasionally label drawings or photos or to make "fun" messages to the family. Obviously for a nonreader, the words will have to be identified each time by you, but if your child glues the word "Godzilla" to paper and then draws a picture, she is apt to remember the word in the future.

Letter Mobiles

A colorful mobile with letters and pictures dangling from it can be a functional and artistic decoration in your child's room. One way to do this is to use a hanger. A colorful plastic one is a good choice, but a wire one can be wrapped in yarn or ribbon first. Then, find a place at the top of the hanger to fix a letter card. This card can be either taped to the hanger or two holes can be punched in it at either side and yarn can be pulled through and tied. Then tie separate strings of yard (make them various lengths) to the bottom rung of the hanger. Attach drawings or photos or magazine pictures (glued on cards) to represent items that began with the letter. From these cards, punch more holes for more strings. Keep the hanger hanging while you're making this mobile, so it can be properly balanced. This kind of mobile doesn't have to focus on phonics, but could be a collection of animal pictures, or baseball players, or just large-size letters (cut from newspapers and mounted on sturdy paper or cards).

4 & UP

SKILLS

✓ Critical thinking

✓ Sorting and classifying

✓ Manual dexterity

27

Trip Souvenirs

SKILLS

✓ **Imaginative thinking**

✓ **Critical thinking**

✓ **Sight word recognition**

✓ **Sorting and classifying**

To commemorate trips your family has taken, give your child the responsibility of collecting "souvenirs" from each trip and preserving them in a handmade book. Punch holes in sheets of construction paper and gather them together with ribbon and yarn. Save ticket stubs, train schedules, brochures, photos, matchbook covers, or restaurant napkins, and help your child glue them into place. If the transportation used was a train, help him find a picture of a train in a magazine and maybe other pictures of tracks, semaphores, and so on. How about finding a suitcase in a magazine, or road signs, or tunnels, or bridges? All of these details can be labeled on each page and provide a graphic memory of each trip. The same idea can be used if you or your spouse are often away on business trips. Simply remind yourself to save stubs and schedules, and when you return, help your child arrange them on paper. The dialogue alone will be worth the effort!

The Joy of Reading

Letter recognition and phonics contribute to the development of learning-to-read skills, but underlying all the technical pieces of beginning reading (and reading throughout life) is meaning. A young child can construct an impressive array of skills and sight words, but without an ability to express and interpret the meaning of print, there is little motivation to read.

This is especially true about literature, and children's literature is a meaningful field, indeed. Reading to your child frequently is the single most important tool for learning to read. Of course, when your child begins to read herself (whether it's actual reading or memorizing a text, or "reading" picture clues), she can "read" a story to you in her own way. The place to start experiencing the joy of reading is at home, long before your child has developed an ability to learn reading strategies, but is able to appreciate stories read aloud.

3 & UP

SKILLS

✓ Imaginative thinking

✓ Critical thinking

✓ Comprehension

✓ Sight word vocabulary

29

dog

5 & UP

SKILLS

✓ Phonics

✓ Auditory discrimination

✓ Sight word recognition

✓ Drawing

Wheel Sound Book

Create a homemade book with an oaktag cover to help with phonics skills. Oaktag can be found in any stationery store. Fold the cover in half and then cut a circle about an inch in diameter on the bottom right of the front part of the cover. On the inside of the back cover, attach with a paper fastener an oaktag circle about the size of the bottom of a coffee can. Make sure this "wheel" turns freely. Staple inside the cover about 6 pieces of white paper, in each of which you have cut a circle that matches the one on the cover. In other words, you've got a book with a hole straight through to the back. Ask your child for a word and its initial sound. She then draws an illustration of the word on the page and you write the initial sound on the "wheel." Then turn the "wheel" to expose a clean space to go on to the next page. When the book is finished, it's fun to turn the wheel and decide if a particular letter fits the picture. Is this a "toy" or "soy" or a "boy"?

cereal

30

Become an Author!

A way to encourage children's interest in books and in the underlying concept that books matter is to make original books at home. There is no limit to the kinds of individual books that can be conceived by you and your child. A sure-fire one could be a book about your child or a pet. In either case, you can begin the dialogue about making a book by talking about the subject and the beginning, middle, and end. These are difficult concepts to grasp for a young child, and often doing is better than planning. A child's handmade book might be only three or four pages, but within this form there will still be a sequence with a beginning, middle, and end. If your pet is the subject, have your child dictate, copy, or write, a sentence or two describing what it looks like. Then, draw and write what the pet likes to eat or play with, and then maybe where it sleeps. These pages can be taped on construction paper. Add a cover with a title and the author's name. Read it from time to time and keep it on a bookshelf with other books.

SKILLS

✓ Imaginative thinking

✓ Language acquisition

✓ Drawing

✓ Inventive spelling

✓ Sight word vocabulary

31

Night-Time Book

SKILLS

✓ Imaginative thinking

✓ Language acquisition

✓ Drawing

✓ Sight word recognition

How about a night-time book? Your child can draw his nighttime rituals on light-colored paper and with your help cut and paste the pictures on dark construction paper. You could use a white crayon to write the simple text on the dark paper or paste a strip of white paper along the bottom of each page so the print will stand out. Another idea is to create a window effect by stapling only at the top another slightly smaller rectangle of black paper onto the large one. On this smaller piece, draw with white crayon or chalk, or glue with construction paper the shape of a window. Leave room under the window for print. The text under this "window" might be a question, such as "What does Jennifer do before bedtime?" When you flip up the "window" there will be a picture on light-colored paper of Jennifer reading a book in bed or brushing her teeth. Finally, the last question on the last page could be "What is Jennifer doing at 9 o'clock?" Flip! And there she is asleep with her stuffed bear.

32

The Play's the Thing

Another way to further an interest in books is to dramatize them. Children and their siblings or friends love to perform shows. Why not suggest a puppet show or simple play about your child's favorite book of the moment? Puppets can be made by drawings on cardboard or construction paper onto which a popsicle stick is glued. You can make a stage by covering a table to the floor with a tablecloth so that the children can kneel behind it and raise the puppets to the level of the table. Scripts for these shows should be kept simple but also allow for improvisation. Children memorize very easily, so a rehearsal or two should suffice if an older child or adult helps organize the production. Nursery rhymes or fairy tales are excellent vehicles for plays for young children. Original scripts are possible, too, if the subject matter is kept concrete; maybe a day in the life of Jennifer or the time the cat was lost, or the day of the hurricane. A wonderful time to perform these entertainments is at family parties or when guests come for dinner with their children.

SKILLS

✓ Imaginative thinking

✓ Language acquisition

✓ Drawing and painting

✓ Small motor development

33

Acting It Out

Another type of dramatic presentation of a story could use the children themselves instead of puppets. And an excellent costume is a paperbag mask! Stick a large brown grocery bag over the child's head and feel underneath for her eyes. Draw a large circle where the eyes are located, remove the bag and cut out the circles. Make sure they're larger than life because the child inside needs really good visibility. All kinds of odds and ends can decorate these masks—cotton balls, strips of yarn or ribbon, colored paper, buttons, pipe cleaners, toothpicks, aluminum foil. As a final flourish, they can be painted, too. Animal books are wonderful vehicles to act out with these masks, especially simple picture books for young children where each animal character has only a line or two to say. Of course, it's not hard to envision Goldilocks and the Three Bears, but a longer story like this requires more children and more organization.

Inventions Galore

Another way to play with the ideas in stories is to have your child create or invent items that are featured in the stories themselves. Suppose you read *The Pied Piper of Hamlin* and you discuss with your child the possibility of a different mousetrap that would capture the mice more efficiently and with less dire consequences to the children of the town, then the means used in the story. Any elaborate or simple mousetrap invention could engage your child's imagination. Cereal boxes, paper towel rolls, string, wire, silver foil, or soup cans, might serve as the materials for the solution to the mice problem, as well as really involving your child in this book.

An indestructible straw house for the one little pig in *The Three Little Pigs* could be a challenge to make, as would a bed that would in no way allow the princess to lose a night's sleep in *The Princess and the Pea*. The list is endless for extending the ideas in popular stories in your own way, and can provide a valuable means for developing and deepening your child's interest in literature.

5 & UP

SKILLS

✓ Imaginative thinking

✓ Small motor skills

✓ Drawing and painting

35

SKILLS

✓ Critical thinking

✓ Language acquisition

✓ Drawing and painting

Opposites

To support the somewhat tricky business of opposites, make an "opposite" book with your child. On a piece of cardboard, oaktag, or construction paper, staple side by side two stacks of white paper that are about 2 inches square. Help your child think of two opposite words like hot/cold, fat/skinny, happy/sad. It might help to begin this activity by reading a book or two with opposites as the theme. The concept is difficult to grasp for a young child, and she will often rely on saying, "not fat" when asked the opposite of fat. But this kind of practice and the actual book made by the child herself will help develop a repertoire of opposite words.

For the book, have your child draw on the left section of the pages an illustration of an "opposite" word such as "fat." Underneath it you or she can write the word. Then on the corresponding page on the right stack of paper she will draw a skinny person, with the word written underneath. Continue on to the next two pages and so on until you have as many words as come comfortably to your child.

TV Smarts

Although it's not always possible to watch a TV show together, planning in advance to do so on a regular basis can contribute mightily to your child's comprehension of what's presented and foster critical thinking skills. Encourage your child to observe and evaluate and form opinions about TV shows, as well as the commercials. This works particularly well when you're watching something together, whether it be good or bad. Asking questions like, "Did you like it?" and then, "Why?" helps your child analyze what you've seen when a commercial interrupts. Draw attention to how loud it is, and have a discussion about why you think this is so. Also valuable in a discussion of commercials is to express opinions about whether it might be true or not. Exploring ideas about TV shows could certainly pave the way toward a family agenda of what to watch and why and, of course, how much, to watch.

3 & UP

SKILLS

✓ Critical thinking

✓ Language acquisition

37

Alphabet Memories

For a simple alphabet recognition game, write all the letters of the alphabet on individual cards and scatter them on the rug or table. Give your child a minute or two to look at the arrangement. (You can place the cards in order for younger children or out of order for a child more familiar with letters.) Then turn a card over and have the child name the letter or cover the letter with a blank card and ask, "What did it cover?" This could be used as a "Concentration" game for lowercase and uppercase letters with all the cards turned face-down. Each person turns over two cards at a time and tries to remember the position of the cards to match uppercase and lowercase letters.

Supermarket Concentration

A different "Concentration" game might consist of a collection of food labels that you've cut out from boxes and removed from cans. When you have two matching ones, glue them on squares of cardboard and when you've got ten or more pairs, you've got a game. The object is to match the labels, but the hidden agenda could be the "reading" or recognizing the names of things. Matching two "vegetable soup" or "oatmeal bread" might transfer over to "reading" the labels in the store or on the kitchen shelf more easily than you think. The format of the labels helps, of course. Your child will associate the colors used or the pictures on the labels, but these are perfectly appropriate reading clues and form a strategy that supports word recognition.

SKILLS

✓ Visual discrimination

✓ Sight word recognition

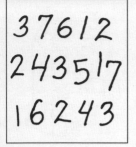

SKILLS

✓ **Sight word recognition**

✓ **Sorting and classifying**

✓ **Graphs**

Size Place

This activity combines both math and reading skills. You can use words from your collection of sight word cards, or you can cut out large-print words from newspaper and magazines. The idea is to count the letters in each word and then glue it on a piece of construction paper under the appropriate number. So when you're cutting out words, make sure some have two letters, three letters, up to five or ten. Spread the words on a table and ask your child to find a two-letter word. Make sure you have a number of each category of words. Ask her to see if there are any more before you move on to the next number. This is really a graph activity, because when all the words are glued, it is easy to see the differences between the lengths of words. If you have more of one category of words than another, you could ask your child which category has the most and which is next.

Homemade Concentration

"**C**oncentration" games, where doubles of every card are matched, are a challenge to play. Cards are shuffled and then laid face-down in even rows while one child at a time tries to remember the placement of cards in the rows. First, he turns over one card and then tries to find its match somewhere else in the surrounding rows. As the game goes on and more cards are turned over, it gets easier to make educated guesses about the location of matches.

You can play Concentration with homemade cards instead of standard playing cards. How about cards with the months of the year on them, or days of the week, or names of all the children in your child's class? All of these are good practice in learning sight words. For younger children, pictures are still best, but you can make cards that have both words and pictures. The words are incidental, but nevertheless provide an opportunity to connect print with pictures of things.

SKILLS

✓ Visual discrimination

✓ Sight word recognition

41

Policeman

SKILLS

✓ Critical thinking

✓ Language acquisition

To develop descriptive language, play the "Policeman" game with a large group of children, such as at a birthday party. One child goes into another room, as the child designated the "Policeman" covers her eyes. Then a third child describes the one who has left to the Policeman and the Policeman needs to guess from the clues. Obviously, the larger the crowd, the harder the game. The clues will start simply; for example, "It's a boy" or "He wears glasses," but can generate much richer descriptions. This game calls upon the observation skills of children as well as memory. The more you model the details of the missing person when it's your turn, the more the children will do the same.

42

Phonics Toolbox

In your hardware store, buy a container with small drawers that is meant for storing different kinds of nails and screws. Make labels out of masking tape for individual initial consonants and fix one on each drawer. Then, to make shopping expeditions more fun for your child, buy a collection of small objects that will fit into these drawers. They're not so easy to find, so the search will be comprehensive and ignite discussions with your child about the best places to look. Obviously, a doll house store is ideal, but maybe too easy. How about a small pencil sharpener for the "p" drawer or a magnet for "m," or a ring for "r"? The hardware store itself has lots of possibilities. The collection might include some familiar foods as well—an M&M, a packet of sugar, a Lifesaver. Each drawer should contain a number of items. The idea is to match the object with its initial sound. From time to time empty them all out on a tray and fill the drawers all over again for a good review.

SKILLS

✓ Alphabet recognition

✓ Phonics

✓ Auditory discrimination

It's a Puzzle!

When your child needs support in recognizing her name, a name puzzle can be a help. Write her name on sturdy paper like construction paper, maybe make a few simple decorations (or your child can do it) and cover it with clear contact paper. Then cut it in jigsaw fashion into 3 or 4 pieces. Your child will enjoy putting her name back together. For an older child, more pieces provide more of a challenge. This puzzle activity can extend to family names as well or could incorporate familiar sight words for a beginning reading activity. It's a good idea in this case to cut each illustrated word into only two pieces. For example, for the word "BOY," print the word on a card with an illustration and then zigzag cut the card between the "B" and the "O."

Library Time

Go to the local library with your child and get him a library card. Find a special place to keep borrowed books at home and have your child write on his personal calendar the return date. The process of choosing books, and of being responsible for their care and for returning them on time is almost as important as reading them! While you're in the library, browse around. Discover which books are in what section, look at the computerized index or the card files, and most important, take some books off the shelves and look at them. When you visit different towns, find out where the library is and pay a visit if you have time. This way your child will soak up the atmosphere of libraries, and he'll be hooked!

5 & UP

SKILLS

✓ **Sight word recognition**

✓ **Visual discrimination**

✓ **Language acquisition**

✓ **Critical thinking**

SKILLS

✓ Phonics

✓ Auditory discrimination

Beginning, Middle, and End

After your child has mastered initial sounds of words, you can move on to middle and end sounds. Make a game with her to see how many of these sounds she can identify. Divide a piece of paper into three columns. Mark one "Beginning," the other "Middle," and the last "End." Give your child a penny to put in the right column each time she answers correctly. Then she can keep the pennies. Call out a letter and a word containing that letter. It's a good idea to make a list of these for yourself, so you'll have a fair distribution of each kind. "Where do you hear the 't' in plant?" or the "'b' in table" or the "'m' in marathon?"

Rhyme Time

Rhyming is another difficult concept for a young child to learn and the skill can be reinforced by making and playing an original rhyming game. Children often consider words that begin with the same sound as rhyming words. With practice they'll discover how the ending sounds creates the rhyme. A good beginning to this activity is to read some nursery rhymes together. To make the game, find pictures or draw on separate cards two words that rhyme, such as "Jill," "hill," "moon," "spoon," "star," "car," "fat," "cat." Cover the cards with contact paper. One way to play this game is to use a "Concentration" format and deal all cards face-down. Keep uncovering cards two at a time until a match is found. Another way is to deal the cards to two or more players, and each player draws a rhyming word from his hand, if he can, to match the card put down by the previous player. As usual, the personal touch of making the game yourselves and creating the picture cards gives the game more meaning and connects it more directly to the child than just buying one in a toy store.

5 & UP

SKILLS

✓ Phonics

✓ Auditory discrimination

✓ Sight word recognition

47

Rhyming Dictionary

SKILLS

✓ Phonics

✓ Auditory discrimination

✓ Sight word recognition

For an older child, you can work on making a rhyming dictionary. The first word in each rhyming pair goes in alphabetical order, so "wing" goes with "w" words and "sing" goes next to it as its partner. Rhyming is an important phonics skill, and making a dictionary can extend your child's repertoire of such words. Depending on the age and interest of your child, this could be an ongoing activity. Staple some paper together and leave some room between each letter so that when you or your child thinks of a pair of rhyming words, or another one that rhymes with a word already in the dictionary you have a place to put it. Obviously, this is also an exercise in putting words in alphabetical order, but don't belabor that part if your child is caught up in the rhyming.

Your Own Comics

Make your own comic book. Look through some published comic books with your child and discuss the format. Point out the symbols used to denote what the characters are thinking; for example, !*x*@! means angry, ? means puzzled. For a younger child a one-page sheet might be sufficient, but a book of a number of pages could also be made. On each sheet of paper draw rectangles for the sequence of the story. In the rectangles, your child can draw the picture and create a bubble in which just symbols are written, or words, or sentences. Words could also be written underneath each picture. The younger the child, the larger the sheet of paper. As in creating any story, the idea of what happens first, second, and so on, should be determined, no matter how loosely, to help your child develop the sense of "story."

5 & UP

SKILLS

✓ Visual discrimination

✓ Sight word recognition

✓ Imaginative thinking

✓ Drawing and painting

Alphabet Antics

SKILLS

✓ Alphabet recognition

✓ Imaginative thinking

✓ Drawing and painting

✓ Small motor skills

Decorating letters is another way to create an alphabet line for the walls or an alphabet book. Help your child make a large uppercase letter on a sheet of paper, and together talk about making something out of it. Animals lend themselves well to this activity, but anything is possible. For example, if the letter is "s," a snake is an obvious choice; "a" could be a house; "b" a person. The drawing shouldn't obscure the letter itself, so the letter probably should be written in a dark marker, and the "decorations" should not include this color. But encourage fanciful designs while reminding your child of the name of the letter she's decorating.

50

Scrambled Sentences

Make some scrambled sentences! When your child is beginning to read, write the words from a favorite short book on separate cards. Then read the book together, the child reading and you supporting him with a few words he might not be sure of yet. Don't pick a book where there are more than two or three of these words. Next, scramble the words of a sentence from the book. Make sure the book is open to that page. It's best to choose a book that only has one sentence on a page. See if your child can put the words back in order using the printed sentence in the book as the model.

SKILLS

✓ **Sight word recognition**

✓ **Comprehension**

Postcard Helpers

Begin a collection of art postcards from museums. Keep them in a special container. Perhaps some of them may be of a painting or sculpture your child has seen in a museum, but the collection can be added to by others as well. Encourage friends and relatives to send such postcards when they're traveling. These cards are good examples of different kinds of art and can generate good conversation, as well as being reminders of visits to museums. Also, they can be used as starting off points for all kinds of creative writing. Consider an American primitive portrait of a child and the kind of ideas it can provoke for a story, or Brancusi's bird, or a Picasso woman. Of course, this postcard collection could also be one of places your child has visited or mixed with places visited by friends. In any case, they should interest your child and serve as topics for creative discussions.

Your Own VCR!

Make your own VCR! Get a medium (no wider than an aluminum foil cardboard roll) cardboard box and place the open end of the box face down. Cut a large rectangle "screen" out of the side of the box that is facing you. On each of the uncut sides of the box, cut a top and a bottom hole that an aluminum foil roll will fit into. Create a long roll of paper by taping pieces of white paper together with clear tape, and with stronger tape attach one end of it to the top roller (or tube) and attach the other end of it to the bottom roller (or tube). Then create a movie or TV show with your child by drawing on each segment of paper. Insert the roller into the holes in the box and your child can narrate the story as someone else turns the rollers, so the "video" changes pictures. You could put subtitles underneath the pictures, but the idea is to have the child narrate the story to an audience.

5 & UP

SKILLS

✓ Imaginative thinking

✓ Language acquisition

✓ Drawing

✓ Sequencing

53

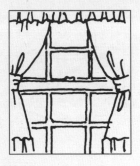

"I Looked out the Window"

SKILLS

✓ **Visual discrimination**

✓ **Sequencing**

A good game to help develop observational skills as well as sequencing skills is "I looked out the window." One person goes to the window and says, "I looked out the window and saw a . . ." and then the next person goes to the window, repeats what the first person said and adds another item. Obviously, the list of what's seen outside the window keeps getting longer and longer and it becomes more and more difficult to remember each item. A good way to organize this game is to determine the number to stop at with the children who are playing. Older children might be able to try for twenty, while younger ones might try for ten. To make it easier, maybe you'll decide the items don't have to be in exact sequence when restated. Also, tell your child that it helps to look out the window for reminders while trying to remember.

It's Time to Shop!

To help your child sort and classify objects and to become familiar with common sight words, make a list with him of the different kinds of stores the family goes to. This might include the shoe store, the hardware store, the computer store, as well as the more obvious food stores. Make labels for each of these stores and then go through magazines with your child and cut out items that can be bought from the various stores. Glue these pictures on index cards and write the name of the object underneath. Spread out the labels of the types of stores and help your child sort what pictures go under which label. Perhaps you could use envelopes marked with each store to keep the picture cards in when the game is finished. This activity could be continually extended as you go through magazines and newspapers and, of course, can be used over and over. Reading the names doesn't need to be pushed, they will become familiar depending on where your child is in the learning-to-read process.

5 & UP

SKILLS

✓ Visual discrimination

✓ Sight word recognition

✓ Sorting and classifying

55

A Book by Its Cover . . .

SKILLS

✓ **Inventive spelling**

✓ **Sight word recognition**

✓ **Imaginative thinking**

✓ **Drawing and painting**

You can recycle book jackets from children's books in a very creative way. Even though your child might know the book that belongs in the jacket, it's interesting to look at the cover together and talk about what other kind of story might go along with it. Could it have the same characters or be in the same place or be silly, or sad? At any rate, the idea is either to create a new story or to extend or change the original one. You and your child can make one up together, or you can take dictation, or your child can write and illustrate one of her own and staple it inside the cover. It helps, even if your child is writing on her own, to talk about the beginning, middle, and end of the story and to ask leading questions about where the story is going. It can be an asset to help guide your child by asking about the characters, or where the story takes place, but remember, if it's her story, you're there to enjoy it, not to write it yourself.

Shoebag Sorting

Shoebags are a very rich resource in your child's room. Each of the pockets can be filed with all kinds of learning materials and can be sorted according to the rules you make up. For example, they can be used for beginning consonant activities, with the letters taped on the pockets and pictures or word cards beginning with each letter stuffed inside. Or, for an older child, you could use the pockets for words that begin with digraphs or speech consonants, such as ch, sh, th, wh, ck, gh, ph, gu, ng, or consonant blends, such as bl, br, cl, cr, dr, fl, fr, gl, gr, pl, pr, sci, scr, sk, sl, sm, sn, sp, spl, st, str, tr, and tw. Another use could be for short and long vowels and the pockets could contain words that either begin with a vowel or have vowels in them. Another use might be to fill the pockets with actual items that match the letters. What about some string for "str" or a "bracelet" for "br" or a toy "umbrella" for "u"?

6 & UP

SKILLS

✓ Phonics

✓ Auditory discrimination

✓ Language acquisition

✓ Imaginative thinking

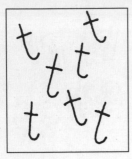

Peter Piper Picked a Peck . . .

SKILLS

✓ **Phonics**

✓ **Auditory discrimination**

✓ **Language acquisition**

✓ **Imaginative thinking**

Make up silly stories that contain mostly words that begin with a specific consonant. Suppose you started it out with "Tiny Tom took a trip to Tibet," and your child could continue it. See how long the two of you can go. You and your child could write down these sentences and stick them into the "t" pocket of the consonant shoebag. Not only does this activity support initial consonant practice, but it also is a vehicle for language enrichment. Searching for more words helps expand your child's vocabulary in a fun way.

Driver's License

I f your child rides a bike, she might enjoy having a driver's license of her own. Both of you can create one, after observing what traditional drivers' licenses look like. Talk about why the information on your license is there and how similar information can be written on your child's license. The bike license can be larger than the usual one for easier reading. Perhaps a young child could copy the information herself. And don't forget a photo, maybe one taken specifically for this license would make it more official. This is a good time to discuss safety tips for "driving" a bike.

4 & UP

SKILLS

✓ Visual discrimination

✓ Sight word recognition

✓ Language acquisition

Vowel Scavenger Hunt

SKILLS

✓ Phonics

✓ Auditory discrimination

✓ Sight word vocabulary

How about a scavenger hunt for vowels? "A," "e," "i," "o," "u," and sometimes "y," can be divided into long and short vowel sounds. "Apple" has a short vowel sound, while "acorn" has a long sound. Long vowels say their name as in Ajax, eject, iris, or ocean. Maybe you could limit the search to one room such as the kitchen or the child's bedroom. Look for only long vowels one time and short ones another time. Perhaps you could write down the words for further discussion. As it is, there will be enough discussion. Scavenging for vowels can be tricky, but it's good practice to see how many words beginning with a vowel you can find.

From "A" to "Z"

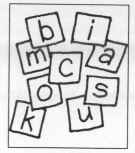

Putting words in alphabetical order can be a challenge. This is an activity for children who have begun to read. It might be good to start off with a children's dictionary and talk about how the words are arranged. Simple questions like "What letter do you think comes in the middle of the alphabet?" or "Which letters are at the very beginning or end?" help focus on the placement of letters. Suggest to your child that she could put all the names in the family in alphabetical order. You or she write them down and cut them into separate pieces. How will you begin? Maybe having an alphabet sight line there will be necessary, but for a child who has internalized the alphabet, it's possible to do it in his head. Keep it simple—the idea is to eventually have a list of 26 words each beginning with a different letter to put in order, but start with small groups. Maybe you could use just middle letters like "k, l, m, n, o," and see how that goes and then gradually extend it to the entire alphabet.

6 & UP

SKILLS

✓ **Alphabet recognition**

✓ **Phonics**

✓ **Auditory discrimination**

✓ **Sight word recognition**

Pack Up!

SKILLS

✓ Phonics

✓ Auditory discrimination

✓ Alphabet recognition

✓ Language acquisition

Play the old game, "I Packed Grandmother's Trunk" as another way to think of words in alphabetical order. One person says, "I packed Grandmother's trunk and put in an avocado," and then the next person says, "I packed Grandmother's trunk and put in a beet." You can do it using only fruit and vegetables, or food in general or any other category. Also, to reinforce auditory memory as well, it's fun to repeat everything that's been said before you add on your own word, but this may be too difficult for young children.

Look! No Vowels!

A good activity to reinforce the importance of vowels in words is to make vowel-less words. Choose a category of words, such as animals. With your help, ask your child to write down many types of animals, but to leave out the vowels. This activity applies to those children who are not only reading, but also have a basic idea of standard spelling. Words without vowels are fundamentally the way children write "inventive" spelling, so it will be interesting to your child to observe the difference between "brd" and "bird" or "hmstr" and "hamster" and to recognize that in writing, she has often left out vowels to expedite things. She still can, but standard spelling is something she can begin to learn as well, and vowels really hold words together.

SKILLS

✓ Inventive spelling

✓ Phonics

✓ Auditory discrimination

Vowel Sort

For more long and short vowel sound reinforcement find ten small containers. One idea is to cut down milk or juice containers of the same size. Cover each with colored contact, or construction paper and write the short vowels on five and the long vowels on the rest. Then with your child, go through magazines and look for pictures of objects that have the different vowel sounds in there. Cut out the pictures, glue them onto index cards or construction paper, write the word underneath or on the back, and put them in the appropriate vowel container. Use this as a sorting activity.

Match Up Blends

Consonant blends are two or three letters blended together, but the sounds are distinct.

To make a game with the most common blends, such as sp, sm, bl, dr, tr, go through newspapers and magazines to find ten illustrations for each, such as shorts, ship, or shirt. Glue the pictures to index cards. Write the blends on as many separate cards as there are pictures. A child sorting this collection by herself can line the blend cards up on the floor and match the pictures to them. A few children at a time could play a game like "Go Fish" with these blend cards.

6 & UP

SKILLS

✓ **Phonics**

✓ **Auditory discrimination**

✓ **Sorting and classifying**

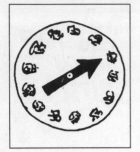

SKILLS

✓ Phonics

✓ Auditory discrimination

Spin a Sound

For a consonant game, trace the bottom of a large pot or dish on oaktag and cut it out. Find small pictures in magazines of common objects that begin with a single consonant, for example, baby, mom, or car. Glue the pictures around the edge of the circle. Place a spinner in the center of the circle. These can be bought in most stationary stores, or you can trace and cut out an arrow and glue a small piece of oaktag in its center before putting a paper fastener in it. The oaktag will elevate the arrow so it can move easily. Children take turns spinning (or your child can play by herself) and saying the initial consonant of word. To make it more challenging, find other pictures that begin with the same consonant, and glue them on separate cards, so that your child needs to find a picture with the same initial sound as the one the spinner is pointing to.

A Sentence Makes Sense

For older children, who have already acquired some sight word vocabulary, it still can be a quandary to figure out just what a sentence is. Cut out letters, words, and sentences from magazines. Divide a piece of paper into 3 columns. Label the first column "Letter," the second "Word" and the last "Sentence." Ask your child to sort individual letters in the "Letters" column, words in the "Words" column, or sentences in the "Sentences" column. First, of course, you need to talk about sentences, and demonstrate that sentences are not just any group of words, but a group that makes sense.

5 & UP

SKILLS

✓ Visual discrimination

✓ Alphabet recognition

✓ Sight word recognition

67

Magnetic Words

5 & UP

SKILLS

✓ Visual
  discrimination

✓ Alphabet
  recognition

✓ Sight word
  recognition

For children just beginning to write or recognize their names, using magnetic letters to match the letters on a name card is a good idea. Try to use a metal tray so the letters stick. Lay the name card (or any other word cards) on the top of the tray and encourage the child to find the magnetic letters that match, and position them under the written letters. Of course, this could also be done on the refrigerator or other metal surfaces if you attach magnetic tape to the back of the word cards so they adhere to the surface. On the refrigerator, maybe food word cards would be a good idea. Your child doesn't need to be able to read each one. It would help to have a picture on it, but if you talk about each word, and maybe make the first sound, matching the letters can be enough. And if the words stay there for a while, there's a lot of opportunity to mention them from time to time so that they will become familiar sight words.

Photo Puzzle

Make a puzzle out of a photograph of your child or another member of your family. Take the photo to a copying machine store and have it enlarged and copied so that it's at least 8" by 10". Then at home glue it to a piece of oaktag. When it's dry, turn it over and draw some lines to create a puzzle. Keep it simple and start with only four or five pieces. Cut them out, mix them up, and put it back together many times with your child.

3 & UP

SKILLS

✓ Visual discrimination

✓ Manual dexterity

Clipping Sounds

SKILLS

✓ **Small motor skills**

✓ **Phonics**

✓ **Auditory discrimination**

Another activity to reinforce beginning sounds uses magazine pictures, alphabet cards, and clothespins! Choose consonants from the alphabet cards that your child is beginning to recognize both as letters and as sounds. Start with no more than eight cards. Either by yourself or with your child, cut out pictures that start with each consonant's sound. Mount these on sturdy paper or oaktag so they can be used many times. Ask your child to spread out the picture cards and the letter cards and match what goes with what: for example, the "f" card and the fish picture. Then use the clothespins (the kind that you can pinch open) to attach the appropriate letter card to the picture card. These clothespins are a welcome addition to an activity and provide an opportunity to develop motor dexterity at the same time.

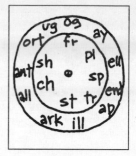

Blend a Word

Cut out 2 different-sized circles to practice consonant blends. For the larger circle, trace a middle-sized pot or plate and use a smaller pot to trace the small circle. Attach the smaller one to the larger one with a paper fastener in the middle. These circles are best made with oaktag. On the edge of the smaller wheel, write some blends with a marker, for example, fr, pl, sp. Word endings can be written on the larger wheel, for example, og, ay, ell. Turn the small wheel and form new words with the different components. It's probably best to make a list of words first that begin with the various blends, so that you don't get too many nonwords.

6 & UP

SKILLS

✓ Phonics

✓ Auditory discrimination

71

Searching for Sounds

SKILLS

✓ Visual
  discrimination

✓ Phonics

✓ Auditory
  discrimination

This is a game for a walk or a ride in the car. One child looks for three things that begin with a certain sound. It's a good idea for someone to time this if a few children are playing. Two or three minutes per object should be enough. Then, if that child finds taxi, a truck, a tree, she gets to pick the next sound for the next child to find. For younger children, look for specific objects, from simplest, such as a dog, or car, to more complicated, such as a girl wearing red shoes, or a dog with black spots, or a man with a mustache. Better not time these!

Lines and Curves

For a younger child who is learning the alphabet, it's a satisfying task to move curves and straight lines around to form letters. Cut out long and short straight lines and big and little half circles from construction paper, and give your child a few at a time. Begin with one long and one short straight line and a small half circle. Ask what letter or letters can be made with the pieces. (Answer, an uppercase "R," and an uppercase and lowercase "p".) This activity reinforces the fact that all printed letters are made of only straight or curved lines.

4 & UP

SKILLS

✓ Alphabet recognition

✓ Visual discrimination

SKILLS

✓ **Inventive spelling**

✓ **Sight word recognition**

✓ **Comprehension**

✓ **Drawing and painting**

Pop-up Books

To encourage your child's interest in creating his own books, it's fun to give books different shapes and styles. One of the best is the pop-up book. The simplest design is to fold a piece of construction paper in half and to cut 2 slits on the fold about an inch or so apart on one side and another 2 slits on the other side of the fold. Open the paper into a tent and push these strips of cut paper through to the inside. Close the paper again and press the cut strip down. Open again to see the pop-up strips pop up! Now, talk about what kind of pictures your child wants to staple or glue on the pop-ups, and what kind of story she wants to write. Cut out some pieces of paper about 2 by 3 inches and ask your child to draw a picture for the pop-up piece for her story. This can then be cut out and pasted or stapled to the raised pop-up. Write the words to the story on the bottom of the page. A number of these pages can be made and glued together to make a book and the cover can be glued on at the end, but it's best not to exceed three or four pages, as the book becomes too bulky.

Shopping List

Compose a shopping list with your child before you both go shopping at the supermarket. For a beginning reader, make some food word cards and have your child illustrate them or cut out appropriate pictures of the food from magazines. Then sit down and work together on the list. "Can you find the "bread" card?" Depending on your child's age, you can either accumulate the cards for the food you need and take them along or your child can write the word on paper for the list. At the store, your child can help be in charge of the list and take out a card at a time for the next selection or read the list with your help.

5 & UP

SKILLS

✓ Visual discrimination

✓ Sight word recognition

Charades

SKILLS

✓ Sight word recognition

✓ Imaginative thinking

Make some cards with simple activities on them, such as "driving a car" or "washing dishes," or "playing tennis." Play a charades game with your child and a few friends, taking turns acting out the movements. Illustrating the cards with a picture of the action might be a good idea, but it's also okay if you or an older child reads the card for a younger one. You could also use animals or favorite characters from books or poems. If you make different categories for this charade game, announce the category before you begin; for example, "this game is only about nursery rhyme characters."

Writing to the Author

Encourage your child to write a letter to her favorite author. If a book by a contemporary author is particularly important to your child, talk about why this is so. Could it be that the character reminds her of someone, or did she find it especially funny or exciting? What about the language in the book? Were there parts that were very beautiful, or was there dialogue that sounded real and familiar? Explore the reasons why the book is a favorite for your child and help her compose the letter. Perhaps she could ask about the author's life and why the author decided to become a writer. Helping your child define what she liked about a book is an exercise in understanding herself better as a reader and can provide more insight into what she is thinking about as she reads a book.

5 & UP

SKILLS

✓ Sight word recognition

✓ Critical thinking

77

Sorting the Mail

SKILLS

✓ Sight word recognition

✓ Sorting and classifying

✓ Problem solving

Sorting the mail is an important task in the family, and your child can help you with the job and learn about the varieties of mail at the same time. Describe the kinds of mail as you sort it together. What might be termed "junk" mail could serve as useful material for making shopping lists with your child or to figure out how much money you can save. Any forms to fill out could provide a lesson in addresses and zip codes and other information. Looking at the dates on the envelope and how many days have passed since it was mailed is also useful. Stamps can be a math problem, as well as an interesting topic for conversation. Help your child establish what the bills, the personal mail, and the magazines are, so that eventually he can sort it on his own.

T-shirt Design

Creating your own design for a T-shirt can establish all kinds of literacy if you use words instead of pictures. All you need is a white T-shirt, some crayons, an iron—and an idea! For a young child, just writing her name on the shirt with a crayon is enough of a challenge, but if your child is older, why not consider a line or two of a poem? Or a series of favorite words, or the name of a special book? All you need to do is press the crayon hard when writing the message and then when it's written, iron it with a warm iron. If you wash the shirt in cold water, the writing should last quite a while. A design or picture might look good with the message, too. If any crayon sticks to the iron, wipe it off while the iron is still warm.

SKILLS

✓ Sight word recognition

✓ Imaginative thinking

✓ Drawing and painting

Personal Tapes

There's nothing that a grandparent or other relative would like more than a tape recording of your child. This tape can be any format. If your child is quite young, maybe you can make the tape together, with you asking questions about things she's done recently. For an older child, it might be easy enough to make an oral letter. In this case, it's a good idea for her to write down a few key words before she begins the tape so she'll remember what she wants to say. A wonderful idea would be for your child to read something. Even if she's mostly memorized a simple text, this is part of the reading process, and showing someone what she can do matters a lot.

Punctuate!

If your child is beginning to learn the conventions of writing at school, here's a good idea for practice. Decide together what you want to work on. Maybe it's contractions, or capital letters in names and places, or even periods. Get out a newspaper or magazine and see if your child can circle whatever you choose to find. This could turn into a counting activity as well. First he could estimate how many periods are on a typical page, circle them, and then count them. Or, he could circle just the capital letters that begin sentences. In a paragraph, he could circle the periods that precede the new sentences as well. It's difficult for children to remember to use punctuation when writing, and this activity can reinforce its importance.

6 & UP

SKILLS

✓ Visual discrimination

✓ Sight word recognition

✓ Critical thinking

81

Book Layouts

SKILLS

✓ Visual discrimination

✓ Sight word recognition

✓ Critical thinking

There are many easy-reader books available that are simple chapter books. All of them have a table of contents in the front of the book. Talking about this page is a valuable lesson in books. Find some other books that have tables of contents. Many children's information books do, but also look at a few adult versions. Even if your child can't read the chapter words, she can read the page numbers and then follow through and turn to the various pages. Depending on your child's interest, you might want to introduce the index, as well. Explain that the words are all in alphabetical order and that you need to look for a key word. For example, say you choose a book about birds. It might be the name of a specific bird, or it might be "wings" or "feathers" that she's interested in. Show her how to find an entry and then help her turn to the appropriate page and find the information with you. Becoming familiar with the layout of books is important at an early age, even if your child can't fully utilize them yet.

Behind Your Back!

A very simple exercise to do with a young child just learning the alphabet is to write on his back! Not with a pencil, but with your finger. This activity could be a follow-up to some work you've done together on certain letters. Tracing them, one at a time on your child's back and having him guess the letter could be an addition to what you've just done. But this is also a great spontaneous activity. Suppose you're stuck in traffic, or waiting in line, or just lolling around the beach? Trace a "z" on his back and then an "x," or maybe you could manage a simple word like "go" for an older child. Try it anywhere, anytime, maybe even when your child is having a bath.

4 & UP

SKILLS

✓ Alphabet recognition

83

Story Jump-starts

SKILLS

✓ Imaginative
  thinking

To encourage your child to write her own stories, you need to draw on a collection of ideas. Talking about monster books, or silly books or books where every sentence begins with the same letter might help inspire her. How about creating a list of opening sentences? "Once upon a time" is fine, but think of others that will help jump-start her writing. For example, "There once was a girl," or "It was a dark and scary night," or "The dog's leash broke and he ran away," or "I know an alien who eats peas." A beginning sentence might be just what your child needs to get going. What about, "I can't think of anything to write about, but the pelican wrote about . . ."?

Personal Favorites

Remember the song in *The Sound of Music* called "My Favorite Things"? All of the things in the song just delight the young woman who is singing. Make a list of words with your child that delight the both of you. The rest of the family could contribute as well, and this could be an ongoing project. What about "frizzle," or "slurp," or "squiggle," or "piano," or "tulip?" Talk about the sounds of words with your child—not so much the components of the word, but the feeling you get when you say it. This interest in words helps children pay more attention to language and certainly helps increase their vocabulary.

5 & UP

SKILLS

✓ **Language acquisition**

✓ **Critical thinking**

✓ **Imaginative thinking**

Love in Bloom

SKILLS

✓ **Imaginative thinking**

✓ **Comprehension**

✓ **Language acquisition**

"**H**ow did your parents fall in love?" is an intriguing topic to talk about or write about with your child. Children are used to hearing family stories about before they were born, but not that many parents think of telling about how they met, what they did together, and best of all, how they felt! This is a marvelously reaffirming story to a child. Hearing about what being in love feels like and how strongly his parents cared about each other from the very beginning is a satisfying tale and one that bolsters his sense of security. Keep it simple: focus on the feelings of wanting to be together with your partner and describe some important highlights about when you met.

Exploring Stories

When reading with your school-age child, discuss the story as you go along. You can talk about characters and how they must feel about something, even if it doesn't say in the book. Talk about who the most important character is and why this is so. You can extend this to your child's reading books, too. In these books, there often is a very obvious main character, but it's a good place to start and then work up to the more complex books that you read to your child. Another area to explore is the problem of conflict in a story. "What do you think the problem is?" and "How does it get resolved?" Thinking about these components of a story helps your child understand how stories are put together and what makes them work. Even at an early age, talking about these subjects can help your child become a stronger reader.

6 & UP

SKILLS

✓ Comprehension

✓ Critical thinking

Reading Strategies

It's important to have some strategies to help your child as a beginning reader. When she is reading to you, have a conversation at certain points about how she is reading the book. For example, pick out a word she has read easily and ask her how she knew the word was "puddle." This helps your child to concentrate on her own reading strategies and explain them to you. Perhaps she'll say she knows "puddle" because it begins with a "p." You can then ask her what other sounds she hears in that word. If she's stuck on a word and the picture can help her make sense of it, point that out to her so she gets used to using the pictures for clues. It will strengthen your child's techniques for comprehension if you ask her to predict what she thinks will happen in a story. After she's read a few pages of a new book, ask her what she thinks will happen to the dog next and why. These strategies will help her become a more competent reader if you include them naturally when you read books together.

Your Own Timeline

A timeline, or a series of dated pictures and writing, can help your child develop a better sense of the passage of time. A particularly appropriate one would depict his life so far. You can use photos or drawings or both, but a good starting off point would be a photo. Suppose it's one of him as a baby and you talk about what he was like then when he was one year old. Later on, when he was a little older, he began to talk, and so on, until your child can begin to remember himself when he was younger. Tack a ribbon on a wall and work backward, illustrating and writing about his life from now to as far back as he can remember. Then you take over and provide details of his life as an infant until the day he was born. When you're done, he'll have a graphic illustration of his life and be able to see better how time changes things. He'll also want to keep adding to it as he grows.

5 & UP

SKILLS

✓ Language acquisition

✓ Critical thinking

✓ Sequencing

Book Publishing

All of your child's books that she's authored are special. Certainly, some of them should go through a publishing process that resembles store-bought published books. This not only will give your child the status she deserves, but also it will help preserve the books. Make a front and back cover of construction paper or colored oaktag and tape the stapled pages inside with wide clear tape. Then the covers should be taped together with colored library tape. She or you can write the title and author on the cover and maybe once again on the inside page. Look at a book and notice the date it was published and the name of the publishing company. Then write your child's own information on the back of the title page. Have your child make up a name for her publisher. Look for blurbs on the back covers of other books. Go over a few of these with your child and help her write her own blurb about her book. Finally, take a photo of the author to glue on the inside the back cover and help your child write a few things about herself for the reader.

Acting Out

Your child must have a lot of favorite books, both the ones he's reading and the ones that are read to him. Make a list of some of them that have titles that could be acted out. This could be done in a charades fashion, with the family guessing the title, or it could be a chance for a few children to dramatize just the title of certain books. Suppose the book is *Cat at Bat* or *The Witch Goes to School* or *Dog*. These and many others can be dramatized, sometimes with words and props or quick costumes, sometimes with only movement and expressions.

5 & UP

SKILLS

✓ Imaginative thinking

✓ Language acquisition

Shopping for Words

SKILLS

✓ **Sight word recognition**

✓ **Visual discrimination**

✓ **Language acquisition**

When you're out shopping with your child, it's a good opportunity to search for words as well as a bargain. Before you go, talk about which stores you're going to and make a short list of words you might find there. For example, if you're going to the drugstore, you might find "paper," "toothpaste," or "hair." In the pet store you might see "cat," "dog," "food," or "tank." Write the words on a piece of paper, and you and your child can look for the words as you stroll up and down the aisles.

Story Dioramas

Sometimes making a diorama of your favorite book enhances the story even more. Suppose your child loves *Cinderella* and *The Trumpet of the Swan*. Think of what particular scenario from the book might be replicated in a diorama. Paint a shoebox both inside and out and then talk about materials that can be used. Maybe a mirror for water, or some small twigs for a broom, cut-out figures, cotton fluff for clouds, and maybe some pictures from magazines. Recreating portions of a book in this way extends its life even more for your child.

SKILLS

✓ Imaginative thinking

✓ Comprehension

✓ Drawing and painting

Washing with Paint

SKILLS

✓ Sight word recognition

✓ Drawing and painting

A clever way to help your young child recognize her name is to do it with secret writing. Use a white candle and write your child's name on white paper with it. Then ask your child to paint the whole piece of paper with a wash of poster paint mixed with water. What happens when the paint covers the letters is the surprise—your child's name appears! Another idea is to ask your child to draw a picture with crayons and to press down on them hard. Then choose one color of poster paint wash and paint over the pictures. All the white bits that went unnoticed are infused with paint, and the overall effect is very attractive.

Music to Paint By

Drawing and painting are the first kinds of writing your child can do. Each piece of work has a message in it, although she might not consciously know what it is. But drawing and painting are expressions of your child's inner life, and children need to be able to experience doing them as much as possible. Children don't need much deliberate inspiration for their work, but sometimes it's a good idea to do something to stimulate creativity. How about painting to music? Put on tapes or the radio and play some different kinds of music while your child paints. A wonderful calming experience could result from a string quartet, and of course, some rock 'n' roll could do the opposite! Experiment with music and painting and after a while your child will be able to ask for certain types of music to paint by.

3 & UP

SKILLS

✓ **Drawing and painting**

✓ **Imaginative thinking**

95

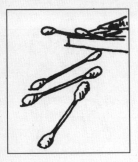

Tips for Painting

SKILLS

✓ Imaginative
  thinking

✓ Drawing and
  painting

There are many different kinds of materials you can use to make a painting. Different-size brushes inspire new techniques, as do a variety of paper and paint. One novelty is to paint with Q-tips. This automatically reduces the broad strokes your child usually makes into something smaller and more precise. How about using small-size paper as well? Perhaps light colored paper and dark poster paints might be a good combination. Q-tips do lend themselves to writing, so your child might incorporate writing into the painting, too.

Letter Writing

Take advantage of those mail order ads for individual name and address stickers, and order them for your child. This could be a wonderful opportunity for showing how to use them in letters to people or even to label things such as books and notebooks. Your child could also use them on her artwork. These labels are good reinforcement for learning your address and are an added attraction for sending mail to someone.

Along with name and address labels, your child might also like to have note paper with her name on it. People don't write letters much anymore, so your child and you can be living proof that it's still a nice way to communicate. Of course, to be a model, you've got to demonstrate that you do write to your friends and also receive letters. There's no better motivation for your child than to realize that letter writing is a natural activity in your house.

SKILLS

✓ Sight word recognition

✓ Language acquisition

✓ Imaginative thinking

Picture Sorts

Make a game for your child that will help him sort and classify all kinds of familiar things into different categories. Suppose you choose the concept "Living or Non-Living" and go through magazines with your child to find examples of each. For example, a tree, a worm, a rock, a pond. Obviously, this could get pretty subtle, so it's an activity for older children as well. You could also categorize "fruits" and "vegetables," "pets" and "non-pets," and the like. Simply cut out pictures, glue them on index cards, and write the word underneath. The cards should include the appropriate label, such as "living" or "nonliving," and your child and you can sort these together. It's a good idea to cover them all in clear contact paper.

Concept Building

One way to sort groups of things that will help concept-building is to make a collection of food, animal, or people picture cards and ask your child to think of ways to sort these according to different attributes. For example, for food, one category could be "color," or "whether a food needs to be cooked or not," or whether it's an "unusual" food or whether "your child likes it or not." These activities offer opportunities for your child to extend the range of her thinking about items that are familiar. Animals could be "hairy" or "scary" "big" or "little," "nocturnal," or "diurnal." Consider as many variations as possible—it's amazing how many there can be!

SKILLS

✓ Critical thinking
✓ Sorting and classifying

99

Written in the Sand

SKILLS

✓ Alphabet recognition

✓ Sight word recognition

✓ Manual dexterity

A multisensory approach to writing and reading is often beneficial to young children. Even children who already know the alphabet and can write it can have their skills strengthened by activities that involve touch. Consider sand writing for learning either letter sounds or initial sounds. Say a letter or a word to your child and ask her to write the letter in a tray of sand, after she first says the sound out loud. You could also ask her to trace the letter in the air, or, believe it or not, in powdered Jell-O for a true multisensory experience.

Touchie-Feelie

A fun activity to help your child practice sound discrimination doesn't just rely on auditory skills, but involves the sense of touch as well. Blind-fold your child and give her an object to feel. When she guesses what it is, she needs to say its name and then the sound it begins with. You could also extend this to middle or end sounds for a child who is ready. Playing this as a game with a couple of children enhances the challenge. Of course, a lot depends on what objects are chosen to feel—a book is fine, but how about a squeeze of toothpaste?

SKILLS

✓ Phonics

✓ Auditory discrimination

Mind-Reading

This activity uses a technique that helps your child internalize writing without depending on only a visual approach. Ask your child to write a particular letter with his eyes open. Then, ask him to close his eyes and write the letter again. This kind of exercise strengthens his ability to "see" the letter in his mind, as well as with his eyes. Do this activity from time to time for a few minutes with your child, particularly if you or his teacher thinks there is any delay in reading skills. But all young children can benefit from it.

Before or After

An alphabet game that helps children order letters both backward and forward reinforces letter recognition as well as the concept that the placement of letters in the alphabet is invariable. Divide up a set of alphabet cards (one of each letter) with your child. The first person turns over a letter and the other person then decides on a letter that precedes or follows it. For example, if you turn over "g" your child can pick either a "h" or an "f." Continue the game until all the letters are used.

SKILLS

✓ **Alphabet recognition**

✓ **Critical thinking**

Letter Matches

To help children learn to match lowercase and uppercase alphabet letters, make individual puzzle pieces of each letter. You can use pieces of construction paper, oaktag, or index cards. On each one, write the lower- and uppercase of each letter next to each other. Then on the back of each, make a simple jigsaw line and cut the card apart. If you can, try to make each line for each card a little different so each card will fit only its match. Make sure you've got an alphabet chart with both lower and uppercase letters nearby for reference when your child does this activity.

104

Rhyming Lotto

To make your own rhyming "lotto" game for a few players, look through magazines for pictures of things that rhyme. For example, a boy and a toy, a tree and a bee. Just be careful to use pictures that are pretty much the same size, about 2" by 2". When you have 32 pictures, 16 that rhyme with 16 others, tape them on a sheet of paper, write the word under each, and make about 20 copies on a copy machine. Then cut all the pictures apart. The next step is to make 4 individual game boards. Each game board should have 12 pictures glued on construction paper, but because you've got 32 pictures, you can vary not only the arrangement on the boards, but each board can have 4 pictures different from the other 3 boards. All the rest of the pictures or cards are used for playing. You could also glue these onto index cards or construction paper. To play, shuffle these cards, put them in a pile face-down and one child reads the cards one at a time. If the other players have a picture on their board that rhymes with the card that was called, they cover that picture with some sort of marker. The first one to cover all the pictures wins.

SKILLS

✓ Phonics

✓ Auditory discrimination

✓ Visual discrimination

Alphabet Tunes

SKILLS

✓ Alphabet
   recognition

Every child knows the alphabet song to the tune of "Twinkle Twinkle Little Star." The difficult part is always when they get to "l, m, n, o, p," and these letters become an indistinguishable mess. This activity can certainly help isolate these letters more, but also it's just fun to try it. Pick a familiar song that your child knows and try to sing the alphabet to that tune. Keep an alphabet line nearby for help, for this can be quite a challenge. Try to find some other song that your child knows and fit the alphabet to them. Maybe nursery rhymes would work for you.

Spin a Letter

To make a game for alphabet recognition, cut out an arrow for a spinner and attach it to the middle of a piece of oaktag where you've drawn a circle. Divide up the circle into 6 or 8 spaces and write a different alphabet letter in each. Make a set of alphabet cards and spread them out. Ask your child to spin the arrow, say the letter it points to, and then pick up the card that matches it. You could also have an alphabet chart nearby for reference. Even though there are only 6 or 8 letters on the circle, it's best to put out all the alphabet cards. You can make more circles and spinners for other letters as well.

4 & UP

SKILLS

✓ Alphabet recognition

Letter Search

SKILLS

✓ Alphabet
recognition

If you're working with your child on
learning the alphabet, one way is to
look for letters on the printed page.
Starting with a child's favorite book is a
good idea. To help isolate the paragraph
or small section of print, take a small
piece of cardboard or oaktag and cut out
most of the center. This makes a frame
for the words. Of course, you could also
choose one whole page of a simple book
and not need the frame. Pick a letter, and
then ask your child to count how many
"p's" she can find. Then ask her to count
all the "s's" and see if there are more
"s's" than "p's."

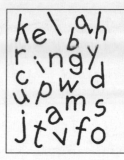

Letter Count

Go through some magazines with your child and cut out about 25 large print words. You could pick them at random, but it would help if some were sight words. Tape them to paper and make about 10 Xerox copies and then cut them apart. Next, write the alphabet at the top of a large sheet of paper. Spread the words out and explain that you're going to look for all the words with "a" in them—not just at the beginning, but anywhere in the word. Glue these words under "a." Obviously, words have other letters that go in different categories, but start with "a" and then search for "b" and so on. Many of the words will be used again and again. After this initial start your child might want to continue finding single words in magazines. It's useful for him to notice that some columns fill up fast because certain letters are common, while other columns are sparse because these letters are less frequently used.

SKILLS

✓ Alphabet recognition

✓ Visual discrimination

Which Is Which?

SKILLS

✓ **Alphabet recognition**

✓ **Sight word recognition**

✓ **Visual discrimination**

For younger children just beginning to get used to print, it still can be a difficult concept to recognize the difference between a word and a letter. When you feel this would be an enjoyable job for your child, make three vertical columns on a piece of paper and label them "Letter," "Word," and "Picture." Write some words the child may recognize (like names) on cards, and also have a set of alphabet cards available. After you've explained what the labels on the paper say, hold up a word card and a letter card and ask "Which one should we put in the Letter column?" Then ask for your child to place it there. For the picture column, you can use magazine pictures or your child can make some drawings on small pieces of paper. The letters and the words and the pictures don't have to relate to each other; sorting out which is which is the point.

Alphabet Word Hunt

Make many different kinds of alphabet lines of words. Suppose you were to find animal words whose beginning letter fit every letter of the alphabet. Or, look around the house and find appropriate words, or go outside. You can start with "a" and work methodically, or you can begin with whatever word your child finds first. Write the word on a small piece of paper when you or child think of one and keep going until you have a collection. Then make an alphabet line on a long piece of construction paper. Spread the words out and help your child find the words for each letter and glue it underneath. You could have multiple words for each letter; then you'll need a larger piece of paper. Still, there will be gaps, and when your child sees the empty columns, see if you can direct her to a place where she can find a word that fits. A dictionary is always a possibility.

5 & UP

SKILLS

✓ Alphabet recognition

✓ Sight word recognition

✓ Language acquisition

SKILLS

✓ **Alphabet recognition**

✓ **Sight word recognition**

✓ **Language acquisition**

Rainy Day Reading

Believe it or not, when you're considering which book to read to your child, a good choice is a dictionary. Many children are fascinated with words when they begin to read and even if your child doesn't seem to fit this description, you could give it a try. Buy (or borrow from the library) a young child's picture dictionary. There are many kinds, from those that are just twenty-six pages long to those that have many words without accompanying illustrations. Start with the simplest one, but if you find you can make it an interesting activity from time to time, get one that's in the middle range. There should be lots of pictures, and the print should be larger than normal. You can start with "a" or even "z" or at a word that is relevant at the moment. Browse through it with your child and read the words and meanings to her. Look at the pictures together and keep a dialogue going. See if she can find a simple word on the page, especially one that has a picture. Don't read them all, but try to intuit which ones interest your child. Keep this book among others as a resource for rainy day reading.

Frames for Letters

Make some small frames out of cardboard or oaktag within which your child can practice writing one letter or numeral at a time. Cut the cardboard into pieces about 4" by 2". At the top of each piece write a number or letter in marker and then underneath cut out a space about 1½" by 1½". Then help your child place this frame on a sheet of paper and ask him to copy the letter in the cut-out space. This activity helps to focus your child's eye on the single letter and removes the "busyness" of a lot of print on the page.

4 & UP

SKILLS

✓ **Eye/Hand coordination**

✓ **Alphabet recognition**

✓ **Critical thinking**

✓ **Language acquisition**

113

Step Up!

SKILLS

✓ Critical thinking

✓ Language acquisition

It is surprisingly difficult to verbalize or write down how to do something. Try this with your child. Brainstorm together how to use the TV, or clean the tub, or play dominoes. If your child is older, think of something with more complicated steps, like making a salad or cleaning a room, or building a sand castle. This is an excellent activity for strengthening logical thinking. How close to the water do you build a sand castle? What steps do you take to clean the salad ingredients? How do you dry them? What about the windowsills? Do you clean them? Help your child write down all the steps and then read them back together. Are any steps missing?

Following Directions

Agood game to develop listening skills in a young child could be played like this. Depending on your child's age, give her some instructions to do a number of things in the order you say them. For example, "Please go open the kitchen door, bring in the broom, and put both the broom and the pepper mill on the doormat." Obviously, all kind of instructions can be given, geared to particular children. You can make a game of it with a few children and they make up the directions for each other. It could get pretty silly, but it's a good memory activity as well.

4 & UP

SKILLS
✓ Critical thinking

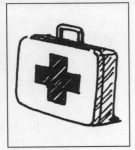

First Aid

A good thing for young children to learn is what people need to do if they get hurt. Talk about this with your child and concentrate on the cuts and scrapes of everyday hurts. It probably goes without saying that an adult needs to administer the "cure." A good focal point is a First Aid Kit, and if your family doesn't have one, this is a good time to start. Take out the various sized band aids and bandages and discuss what they could be used for. Describe how and why the antiseptic is used, and the antibiotic cream. This is also a good time to take out your choice of children's pain reliever and discuss with your child why it's used, and also how important it is that it never be taken by a child alone. The thermometer should also be explained and maybe a medicine that soothes tummy aches. And don't forget to talk about the need for that other important medicine— soap and water.

What's That?

This is a good activity that promotes observational skills. Get a roll of film and take some photographs of objects and places that are in your child's environment. But don't be obvious—pick things that aren't necessarily that noticeable, like a small plant behind the others on the windowsill, or the door on the side of the garage, or the view of the telephone pole from the hall window. It's fascinating to discover what's familiar to your child, and she will want to use the camera to see if she can trick you or other family members.

SKILLS

✓ Visual discrimination

✓ Observation

Spread the News

Help your child create her own bumper sticker. Look around and see what's out there and then do some brainstorming of your own. You can make a personal one, like "I Love Midtown West School" or a political one like "We Need a Woman President," or what about "I Love Mom"? Figure out with your child what size paper fits on the bumper and then write the message on construction paper and cover both sides with clear contact. Then glue or tape it onto your car and spread the news.

Homophones

For an older child, finding words that sound alike but mean different things can be an intriguing job. Maybe you can just keep a list on the refrigerator and you and all the members of the family can contribute the words over time. Your child should be at least a beginning reader, but the list doesn't have to have only words he can read. The point is to establish the fact that there are such words (homophones) so that eventually your child will recognize some on his own. What about "hair" and "hare" or "one" and "won" or "sew" and "so"?

SKILLS

✓ Phonics

✓ Auditory discrimination

✓ Language acquisition

✓ Sight word recognition

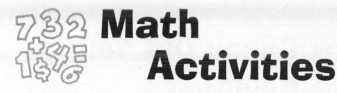

Math Activities

Providing a welcoming climate at home for math activities depends on viewing math as more than the arithmetic skills of addition and subtraction, and not only as working with numerals, which are only symbols for actual things. Math for young children needs to be concrete, not symbolic. Sorting and classifying things is the first step toward observing the similarity and differences between objects and to organize objects according to their attributes, such as size, color, or shape. By using real objects, such as beans, toothpicks, and buttons, your child can build a foundation of math concepts that she can later express in numbers. Using her senses to solve math problems enables your child to represent abstract concepts in a hands-on way that she has control over. Although it is important to recognize written numbers and there are many activities you can do at home to help your child learn them, the real emphasis on early math skills should concentrate on using tactile materials to explore problem solving.

Check Out Your Room!

SKILLS

✓ **Sorting and Classifying**

✓ **Drawing and painting**

✓ **Observation**

Sorting and classifying your child's room can be an introduction to logical thinking. Clean-up time can be a welcome version of this activity, but you can do a less physical version by simply sitting in the room and looking at and describing the objects that you see. Notice all the similarities and differences of the different toys, furniture, clothes, and so on that are in the room. Make a list and have your child draw the different items and then sort them into different qualities, such as hard/soft, big/small, heavy/light, or colors.

Number Lines

Make number lines by cutting out old calendar numbers and putting them on a tray or table. Depending on your child's readiness, you might sequence the numbers, or put out only five or ten at a time, or put them all out at once (right side up). The child glues the numbers in order on strips of colored paper. It helps if paper strips are not too long (holding not more than ten numbers), so the task is not daunting and also because children feel very accomplished if you or they need to keep stapling additional strips to each other. Keep in mind that for older children cutting the numbers apart (29 becomes a 2 and a 9) can allow them to continue the number line up to a 100 . . . or?

5 & UP

SKILLS

✓ **Numeral recognition**

✓ **Counting**

✓ **Sequencing**

Make a Calendar

SKILLS

✓ Numeral
  recognition

✓ Counting

✓ Patterns

✓ Sequencing

By cutting out an assortment of old calendar numbers, children can make their own monthly calendars for themselves. You or your child can draw the grid for a month and fill in together the name of the month and the days of the week. Then, by copying an entire existing calendar, the child can glue the numbers in the appropriate spaces. Another option is to glue the numbers in daily. An even simpler format is to roll a small piece of masking tape and attach it to the back of the number instead of using glue. This way the numbers can be recycled. The calendar could be taped to the refrigerator or some other busy place and filled in at some point during each day.

Really Counting

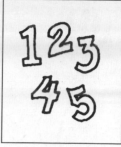

"**C**ounting," or being able to recite numbers in sequence, is different from understanding how to count objects. The latter skill relies on a child's ability to use one-to-one correspondence. The difference is easily seen when a young child "counts" a row of crayons or small animals. It's very common for the numbers to be recited correctly, but various objects along the way to be skipped over entirely.

Depending on the developmental level of your child, begin to count familiar items at home. For some, it might be appropriate to count the three spoons on the table or the four toys in the bathtub. Make counting an ordinary activity, done spontaneously at all sorts of times. This is easy when setting the table, folding the towels, or putting the stuffed animals to bed. But it can extend to counting all the doors in the house, the chairs in a room, the plants, or the windows. To make it a bigger challenge, count all the red objects in the room. You judge how comfortable your child is counting and how to extend her range without pressuring her.

3 & UP

SKILLS

✓ One-to-One correspondence

✓ Counting

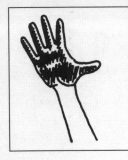

Counting Hands

At job lot stores or at stationary stores, it's possible to buy rolls of white paper that are wide enough for a child's hand print. A fun (and not too messy) activity is to make a line of hand prints under or over which a number is printed. This type of number line is quite decorative and can be hung along the top of your child's bedroom wall as a resource.

Gather some sponges and paper towels, and spread the rolled paper across the edge of the table or along the floor on top of newspaper. Taping it at each end should help keep it from sliding around. Use at least two or three different colors of tempera paint. Pour just a little of each color in flat serving dishes or trays, just enough to coat the bottom. Have your child place her hand flat in the layer of paint and then lay her hand on the white paper. Lift upward carefully and you've got a print. Then you or she can paint the number under it. Going up to ten makes quite a respectable length, but how about fifteen or twenty?

Button Number Lines

Another kind of number line goes in a vertical direction. On a sheet of construction paper mark off ten lines and write the number 1 in the first space and continue until you reach 10. Put a collection of odd buttons and some glue out and help your child match the appropriate number of buttons to the numeral. This activity is the next step up from much simpler one-to-one correspondence tasks such as setting out one cup for every child for snack, or placing one paintbrush in each paint container. The number line matches one-to-one, but requires numeral recognition as well. One-to-one correspondence is a fundamental math concept that is still being developed in a young child. Observe if your child has difficulty matching the buttons to the numerals. If this is so, do some simpler activities like putting out a pile of ten pennies and a pile of ten small plastic animals. Ask the child if there are enough pennies for each animal if each animal costs one penny. Exercises of simple matching like this one builds competence for completing the number line.

SKILLS

✓ **One-to-One correspondence**

✓ **Numeral recognition**

✓ **Counting**

Juicy Counting

To make a simple one-to-one correspondence game, collect ten small juice cans. Cover each in colored construction paper. Then on each can color in with a marker dots from 1 through 10. Use a domino pattern for the dots. Collect 55 popsicle sticks and ask your child to match the number of possible sticks to the number of dots on each can and fill the can. You could vary this game by using buttons or pennies.

To ensure a long life for this game you can cover each can with clear contact paper. Of course, you can extend the number of cans to twenty or twenty-five, but the popsicle sticks won't fit, so pennies or small counters must be used instead.

Match the Number

Make some number cards with your child. (These cards can be used in numerous activities, so even if you write the numbers on index cards instead of construction paper, it's best to cover them with clear contact paper.)

For a younger child who is beginning to recognize written numerals (but not yet writing them as easily) put out cards numbered 1 to 10 on a table. Assemble a collection of similar objects, such as pennies, small blocks, dried beans, or buttons, and ask the child to count the appropriate number of objects to match each numeral card. If you like, you can make large number cards so that the objects will fit onto the card itself.

4 & UP

SKILLS

✓ **One-to-one correspondence**

✓ **Counting**

Secret Numbers

6 & UP

✓ Counting

✓ Critical thinking

Play a secret number game! This activity reinforces the math skills "bigger than" and "less than." Before you begin, talk to your child about the terms. For example, ask your child if 4 is bigger than 5 or less than 5. These skills can be a little wobbly, but practice them so your child will enjoy the game.

To start, one child chooses a secret number. For younger children, stick to numbers 1 to 10. The other children take turns asking questions. For example, "is it bigger than 3?" "Is it less than 10?" The secret number child then answers yes or no, and eventually someone will guess the secret number. Another way to play this game is to have the guesser simply give out a number and then the "secret" child provides the clue; for example—"7 is 'more than' the secret number" or "1 is 'less than' the secret number." When a child guesses a number and the "secret" child says her number is "bigger than" or "less than" that number, the child who guessed covers that number on a number line. This way the choice is narrowed in a graphic way.

Roll a Number

To make a dice game, fold a piece of paper into six vertical columns and draw six or seven horizontal lines across the paper. Write at the bottom of each column the numbers 1 to 6. Give your child one die and when he rolls a number, ask him to color in a segment in the appropriate number column. For example, if he rolls a 4, he would then color one segment of the "4" column. This could be a game to play alone, but if the competitive urge is upon you, you or anyone else could join in and have separate sheets. Then the idea could be that the first person who colors all the segments wins the game. This is a good activity for visual discrimination, and it helps a young child understand that the arrangement of dots on a die represents a number. There are also dice you can buy that have numerals instead of dots on each side. These are useful when a child is beginning to recognize numerals. It's important to remember that for the dot dice a child will probably need to count the dots for a while before the configuration becomes familiar. Photocopy these sheets so that it can be an ongoing game.

5 & UP

SKILLS

✓ Numeral recognition

✓ Counting

✓ Visual discrimination

Repeat!

SKILLS

✓ Patterns

✓ Eye/hand coordination

A simple way to begin arranging things in a pattern is to make a paper chain or thread beads for a necklace. Start with two colors only. Ask your child to think of a way to make the chain or necklaces so that the colors will keep repeating. For young children this takes some practice, so limiting the colors makes it do-able. Talk about how this can be done, and before making the chain or necklace, practice putting the colors in a pattern first. If you put one yellow out and then one red, what should come next? And next? Use the word "repeat" when demonstrating. When the idea seems clear, the child goes ahead and folds and glues the paper strips or threads the beads. The next time around the pattern can be more complex, for example, two red, one yellow, and so on. Obviously, the paper chains can be used as decorations for holidays and such. Your child might help you cut the strips. You or she can also use a ruler to draw the lines. But they don't need to be perfect!

Pattern Rubbings

To further develop observation of patterns, look particularly close at floors and walls with your child. The bathroom especially is often a wonderful source of tile patterns. Some old tile floors used only hexagonal tiles and sometimes have borders of different shapes. Tile walls, like brick walls, follow certain basic arrangements that are repeated over and over.

A good activity to do to extend this pattern search is a pattern rubbing. Take some ordinary white paper (large easel paper would be best) and lay it flat on the floor. Ask your child to remove the paper from a crayon, and holding the crayon lengthwise, rub it all over the paper to expose the pattern underneath. For tile or brick walls, tape or hold the paper while your child makes the rubbing.

5 & UP

SKILLS

✓ Patterns

✓ Eye/hand coordination

131

Symmetry

SKILLS

✓ Patterns

✓ Drawing and painting

Another way of seeing patterns is to create symmetrical designs. This activity doesn't extend a pattern more than once, but it does introduce a new idea and the word *symmetry*, and it's also a fulfilling art experience. No need to talk about it in advance, but when the patterns are done, remark on what you see. "Is this one the same as the other?" "What about the color here—can you find it on the other side?" "Does this pattern repeat?"

You need poster paint and light-colored construction paper for this activity. Use only three or four colors at one time, otherwise it will be difficult to see the pattern for beginners. Fold the paper in half and open it up. Ask your child to splash (gently) a drop of different colors all over one side of the paper. Then carefully fold over the other side, press, open, and voilà—symmetry! Practice using small brushes and small drops or just a few large drops, and see what happens. When dried these designs are framable, or in smaller sizes make wonderful greeting cards to send to friends and relatives.

Natural Symmetry

Another experience in symmetry is to look around your environment for examples. A good place to start is the child herself. Use a mirror and ask the child to draw an imaginary line down her middle from top to bottom (use your finger to demonstrate). Are the sides the same? Open your mouth and let the child examine your teeth. Are all the big ones (molars) the same on each side? Continue this activity with the rest of the body.

SKILLS

✓ Patterns

✓ Observation

✓ Critical Thinking

Look for other symmetrical patterns both inside and outside. Are there designs in rugs or on pillows? Is the stove arrangement symmetrical, or the faucets on the sink? What about patterns on dishes or an arrangement of windowpanes?

Then check nature. Look at leaves, there's a line down the middle and identical sides. What about flowers, buds, and other animals or trees? Symmetry is a natural design, although it isn't always absolutely perfect. It's a valuable idea for your child to experience what a common form it is in the world. Equally important is a discussion about why they think this is so.

Fingerprints

Take your fingerprints! Press your thumb and your child's thumb onto a stamp pad and stamp the print on a piece of paper. Using a magnifying glass will help the pattern be clearer. First of all, is there a pattern of lines? Is the pattern symmetrical? How do thumbs compare with pinkies? Is your thumb print identical to your child's? Even without discerning every line, it is an interesting experience to observe the patterns, the similarities, and the differences in everyone's fingerprints. You might try this with toes as well. And, of course, if your child is old enough, talking about why criminals are fingerprinted is relevant.

An arrangement of your child's fingerprints, or those of the whole family could make a very creative greeting card.

Design a Pattern

Attractive pattern designs can make interesting art as well as support mathematical thinking. Consider what you've got around the house that a child can use in gluing together a pattern. Pieces of fabric, macaroni, beans, colored paper, scraps of wallpaper, stickers, decorative stamps, magazine pictures, even letters and numbers might all contribute to various pattern activities. Encourage your child to arrange his display on a strip of paper first without glue to check out if the pattern repeats. A useful way to do this is to set up a rhythmic "naming" of the pattern: "1 Macaroni, 1 black bean, 1 macaroni, 1 black bean . . ." establishes the repetition of the pattern orally. All kinds of original and dynamic patterns can be created using found materials and many can be functional as well—book covers, bookmarks, place mats, greeting cards can all be examples of original patterns.

As for letter and number patterns (1, 2, 3, 1, 2, 3; Aa Aa B, Aa Aa B), these can strengthen writing skills and number and letter recognition as well as support the basic patterns arrangements.

SKILLS

✓ Patterns

✓ Numeral recognition

✓ Alphabet recognition

Building Patterns

SKILLS

✓ Patterns
✓ Eye/hand
   coordination

Patterns can be created by using familiar toys in a mathematical way. If your child has a pegboard and colored pegs, you can make varied patterns on them. Blocks of different sizes or shapes can be arranged in vertical or horizontal patterns. Pegs and blocks make wonderful pattern arrangements, and so do Lego®. You might build a Lego® road using a particular pattern or create a symmetrical figure or other construction using Lego®s. Many kinds of small manipulative materials are ideal for these activities and using them as mathematical tools adds a valuable dimension to them.

Pasta Patterns

Noodle necklaces or pasta patterns are fun to make and are also exercises in pattern making. Pick your noodles, maybe ziti, or large penne, or elbows, or maybe a combination of two or three. Get some plastic cord from a handicraft store or just use yarn. Have a few containers of water out, and into each squeeze a few drops of different food colors. Your child can then choose which noodles to dip into which color, or just alternate color with the same shaped noodle. Use a slotted spoon for dipping and then lay the colored noodles on paper towels to dry. From time to time, check that the noodles aren't sticking. Then string the pasta into patterns for jewelry. These necklaces and bracelets are not meant to last forever but certainly can be worn for a day or two. For longer lasting pasta patterns the noodles can be glued on paper into patterns instead.

5 & UP

SKILLS

✓ Patterns

✓ Eye/hand coordination

SKILLS

✓ Counting

✓ Collecting and recording data

Count and Record

Make a family or a friend "jumping survey." Help your child write the names of all the jumpers (or hoppers) and then see if each person can jump twenty times (or ten, or twenty-five, etc.). Keep records like these on a clipboard. Think of other counting activities for the family. Count and record the number of letters in each person's name, the different ages of everyone, how many times each person can jump rope or bounce a ball. Put the timer on to see how many minutes it takes for each person to take a bath, walk the dog, or speak to Grandma on the phone.

Egg Carton Math

Egg carton math is fun. With a marker write numbers 1 to 12 in each cup of an egg carton. Have an assortment of pennies, beans, buttons, etc. and help your child count the appropriate number of objects for each space. Practice with her at first, and for each number count out loud, for example, "1, 2, 3, 4, 5." It might help if you arrange the correct number of items in advance (78). This way it will be easier to know if the counting is accurate because there will be no objects left when 12 cups are filled. Still, counting them with your child is the only way to be sure.

For another level of math activity, the egg carton could serve as a simple addition game. In each cup of the carton write a simple equation or number sentence, such as 1 + 1 = 2, 1 + 2 = 3. Then help your child add the two groups together for the sum.

SKILLS

✓ **One-to-One correspondence**

✓ **Counting**

✓ **Numeral recognition**

Number Books

SKILLS

✓ **One-to-One correspondence**

✓ **Numeral recognition**

✓ **Counting**

✓ **Drawing and painting**

✓ **Eye/hand coordination**

Make a number book with your child. Fold six pieces of paper in half and staple along the edge to make a book of twelve pages. Either you or your child can write the numerals and your child can draw the accompanying number of objects. Depending on your child's ability at the time, decide what numbers might provide a challenge and be around to help.

If your child would like to glue objects such as buttons, toothpicks, paper shapes, or magazine pictures, make sure you keep the pages separate before you assemble the whole book so the glue doesn't stick all the pages together.

Surrounded by Numbers

Recognizing numbers in the environment is an important step in understanding the role of numbers in our lives. Do this activity in various ways. One way is to simply notice numbers and talk about them. Look around the kitchen and find examples of numbers (the clock, the dial on the refrigerator, on the timer, on the calendar, etc.). Or you could extend this activity to any room.

Another way, generally for older children, is to ask them to find a particular number, for example, a 12 (on the TV dial) or a 9 (on the cereal box). A much more graphic way to do this activity is to write the numbers down and ask the child to find them around the house. Your child should then write down, or draw, the location of the number, either on her own or with your help. This activity can become quite fascinating when you begin to discover all the places numbers exist, such as inside a shoe, on a stamp, or on a candy wrapper.

5 & UP

SKILLS

✓ Numeral recognition

✓ Observation

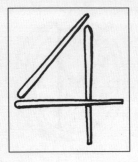

A Four's a Four

SKILLS

✓ Numeral recognition

✓ Counting

✓ Eye/hand coordination

Young children often think that individual numbers are static, that is, that a 5 or a 7 can't be represented in different ways and still be a 5 or a 7. To experience that a number remains the same in any arrangement, ask your child to use only toothpicks but on separate index cards to make a 4 a different way each time. For example, 4 could be arranged as a house shape, and 4 could be a straight line. Obviously, the possibilities increase with different numbers. Count along with your child as she arranges (and glues) different configurations of 3 or 8. Avoid the possibility of just clumps of toothpicks by emphasizing arrangements and by demonstrating some of your own.

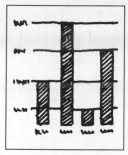

Graph Away!

Graphing helps children understand and actually see relationships between things. Simple ones can include a birthday graph, a comparison of two or three favorite foods, or a simple "yes" or "no" graph. The layout can be flexible, but a common type lists information across the top and along the left side, and lines are either colored or glued across to record the results. For example, a birthday graph might list the months across the top and names of family members along the left side. If Mom's birthday is in April, a line from Mom's name is drawn across until it reaches April. A favorite food graph would list "pasta," "broccoli," and "chicken." The food can be listed across the top and names of people on the left side. A simpler "yes" or "no" graph can be designed with a question across the top and people's names on the left. Under the question write "yes" or "no" and people can make a check accordingly.

When the information is on the graph, it is important to observe and discuss the results. "How many birthdays in June, or February?" "Which column has the most, or the least?" and so on.

5 & UP

SKILLS

✓ Graphs

✓ Critical thinking

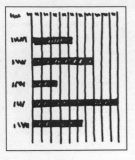

Daily Graph

A visual interpretation of how many hours your child spends each day (and night) doing various activities can result in an interesting graph. Start this task by agreeing that there are 24 hours in every day and that certain activities take up a particular number of hours every day. You might write down the numbers 1 to 24 across a piece of paper and then begin to talk about or write down the kinds of things that happen every day in your child's life. Keep to big blocks of time, not short ones, and narrow the list to such things as eating, being in school, doing homework, playing, traveling, sleeping. With the number line of 1 to 24 on top of the paper, write down on the left side all the activities you've chosen, such as sleeping, school, or riding on the school bus. Either color a line across for the number of hours spent doing the activity or glue strips of paper instead. It really is so that nine hours are spent sleeping, and six are spent in school. Finally, add up the hours and see how close you get to completing an average or typical day.

Tracing Shapes

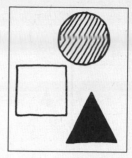

Young children love to trace shapes, either by tracing around the outside of a shape, or by tracing along the inside of a stencil. Along with developing better small motor skills, tracing is a big boost to learning basic geometrical shapes. To make stencils, use pieces of cardboard and outline and then cut out a triangle, a square, a rectangle, and a circle. Don't discard the "insides" of these stencils, as they become figures to trace around. In the beginning, help your child to place her one hand flat down on the shape or stencil to hold it fast while tracing with the other. This is an important first step, and sometimes it's useful to help hold it down with her. A useful activity with these stencils and shapes is to make a shape book. After your child is finished tracing a shape, help her cut it out and then glue it to a paper. You, or she can copy the name of the shape, and when all four are done they can be stapled into a book. But don't think it's over with one book! Children will trace and then color in the shapes for a long time.

4 & UP

SKILLS

✓ Geometric shapes

✓ Eye/hand coordination

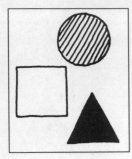

Shape Hunt

An activity that helps identify basic shapes is a shape hunt (the kitchen is a wealth of shapes), or just go along with your child throughout the house. A simple way for a young child to keep count of how many shapes he finds is for you to draw the shapes along the side of a piece of paper. When the child discovers a particular shape, he writes a tally mark. For older children, writing down the information can be added. Aside from counting up the tallies, the triangles, or circles, this activity really draws attention to how common the basic shapes are in our environment.

Sponge Printing

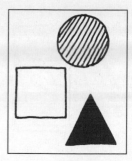

For a colorful painting activity, as well as one that reinforces basic shapes, cut two or three different kinds of triangles, circles, squares, and rectangles from new sponges. Place a layer of poster paint in trays or platters and put two or three of the shapes in each one. Using the primary colors makes an attractive combination on white paper. Show your child how to hold the sponge shape carefully around the edges and to dip it into the paint carefully. Then show her how to stamp the sponge onto a piece of paper. The idea is to stamp it once, and not to rub it around, so the outline of the shape is pretty clear. The first print is always very full of paint; encourage your child to continue to print without placing the sponge back into the paint for a while. This creates an interesting textural effect. Make sure you discuss as you go along the various shapes that are being used, and when the work is dry talk about and count the triangles, squares, rectangles, and circles that are on each paper.

SKILLS

✓ Geometric shapes

✓ Imaginative thinking

✓ Eye/hand coordination

Geometric Art

SKILLS

✓ Geometric shapes

✓ Imaginative thinking

✓ Eye/hand coordination

Make a paper shape box for all kinds of shape activities. Cut out a number of squares, rectangles, triangles, and circles from various kinds of construction paper. Put them all in a box to use for collage work. Your child might like to make animals from the shapes. Another good activity is to read a simple story and work with your child to create scenes from that story using only the four basic shapes. Of course, it is a boon to have all sorts of sizes and types of the shapes to give enough variety to this activity. Imagine the bears going for a walk, or Goldilocks sleeping on the little bear's bed, all constructed of geometric shapes. These shapes are also good for a number book or for making patterns.

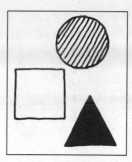

Bag It!

A guessing game for learning and reinforcing basic shapes can be fun. Take various objects that are the four basic shapes and put them in a bag. Have your child or children take turns dipping into the bag and selecting one item. While still holding it inside the bag, ask your child what shape it is. After he answers, he then removes it from the bag and sees if it's right. The simplest way to do this game is to use various shapes from toys your child might have, like pattern blocks, or game pieces of the basic shapes. To make it more of a challenge, select items around the house, after first explaining that the shapes will be solid ones, not flat ones like the game pieces.

4 & UP

SKILLS

✓ Geometric shapes

✓ Critical thinking

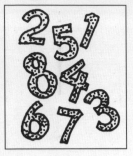

Sandpaper Numerals

As with alphabet letters, making numbers out of sandpaper and using them for numeral recognition is a good idea. Buy some coarse sandpaper and number stencils at a hardware store. Outline each numeral on a piece of sandpaper and cut them out. Mount each numeral on a sturdy piece of cardboard or oaktag. Encourage your child to feel the number with one finger and model how you do it as you write it. Perhaps you might guide her finger around each numeral as you say its name.

One activity that's fun is to ask your child to close her eyes and try to guess which number she is holding by feeling it with her fingers.

The Bigger the Number . . .

To discriminate between greater and smaller numbers, play this game with a deck of cards with two people. Use only the ace through 10 of a deck of cards. Shuffle and deal the same amount of cards to each player and keep them face down on the table. Each player turns over one card at the same time, and the person with the greater number takes both cards. If both cards tie, each turns over a second card. When all the cards have been played, each player counts his or her cards, and the player with the most cards wins.

5 & UP

SKILLS

✓ **Numeral recognition**

✓ **Critical thinking**

Beginning Measurement

SKILLS

✓ **Measurement**

✓ **Estimation**

✓ **Eye/hand coordination**

✓ **Making comparisons**

For a young child, measuring things with standard measurements using rulers and yardsticks is too abstract. It's best that they approach measurement by using nonstandard methods first. Paper clips, lengths of string, crayons, feet, and beans are all good measurement tools. Choose two or more of these objects and look around with your child to find things to measure. If your child can work independently, create a "picture" list of items she can measure around the house, and ask her to record how many beans or paper clips long the TV, refrigerator, bookshelf, or a sneaker is. Talk about the findings when she's done. Why is it that the number of beans is less than the number of paper clips used in measuring anything? Do you think that if you measured with crayons and beans there would be more crayons or more beans? If you use your own feet to measure a rug, why is it that the number of your child's feet is larger than yours? Measuring with these nonstandard units prepares the way for centimeters and inches, and also gives your child opportunities to compare and see relationships.

Turn Up the Volume!

Another way to compare measurements, this time with volume, is to use different-size jars and some rice. This activity has a mess component, so make sure you place the jars and rice on a tray or in a plastic storage container to catch spills. Just experiencing pouring the rice and noticing when to stop is a good first activity. With a permanent marker draw a line around various jars at different levels. Find some measuring scoops or use coffee scoopers to scoop the rice into the jars up to the black line. Young children are entranced with this activity and will repeat it over and over as they gain more dexterity and confidence. Another way to use jars and rice is to ask your child to fill one jar to the top and then pour the contents into a jar of another size. Was there too much rice, too little, or just enough to fill the second jar? In this way young children make comparisons and draw conclusions about volume.

SKILLS

✓ **Measurement**

✓ **Small motor development**

✓ **Making comparisons**

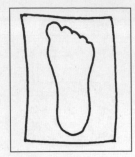

SKILLS

✓ **Measurement**

✓ **Making comparisons**

Footloose

To develop the concept of comparison, ask your child to trace on paper each person's foot in your family. You could include other friends and family as well if you want a bigger picture. When the foot is traced, write the person's name inside it and help your child cut it out. Spread the feet on the floor and look for the biggest, the smallest, the next smallest, and so on. Arrange them in order on the floor or glue them on large sheets of paper. Throughout this activity, keep up a conversation about the feet: for example, Meg's foot is smaller than Anne's, Mary's foot is the biggest, yours is in the middle. This will help your child learn to sight read names, as well as develop spatial relationships.

Measuring Ourselves

You know the body outlines of children you often see in school? Well, if you have a roll of brown paper, this is always an entertaining activity to do at home. If you have a large roll of brown paper, you could help your child outline every member of the family and then with their help, color in the clothes, hair, and so on. These outlines could be used for a measurement activity, if you've got the space to lay them out in a row and compare sizes (outside is a good idea if you've got a large family).

SKILLS

✓ **Measurement**

✓ **Making comparisons**

✓ **Drawing and painting**

Family Measurements

SKILLS

✓ Measurement

✓ Making comparisons

Another way to compare size is to give your child yarn or a roll of adding machine paper to measure each person in the family. Everyone should lie on the floor for this, as your child extends the length of yarn or paper from the feet to the head. If she's used the paper, help her write the person's name on it, and with the yarn, attach a piece of masking tape around it and write the name. Then lay them all out and find out who's the tallest, shortest, and so on.

Food Sort

A good sorting and classifying activity is sorting food into groups. Cut out pictures of all kinds of food from magazines. Depending on your child's ability, you might do most of the cutting, but some should be done together so you can talk about the various foods as you go along. When they're all cut out, mix them up and begin to sort them into categories. You need to decide with your child what these categories should be, but in general you might use dairy foods, vegetables, fruit, meats, fish, bread, and desserts. You could have pieces of construction paper of different colors for each category and spread them out, or you could just pile them onto trays or paper plates that have the category name written on them. Your child might want to glue the arrangements onto the paper, or you could mix them all together again to be used for sorting at other times.

5 & UP

SKILLS

✓ **Sorting and classifying**

✓ **Small motor development**

Estimates

To really comprehend what a number is takes some time. One way to increase this understanding is to estimate amounts. If you check your estimates by counting the objects afterward, you help develop sound number sense. Estimating must make sense. If a child estimates wildly, it shows that her perception of what a number actually represents is off and she needs to practice in forming a more accurate picture over time. An estimate is an educated guess.

Opportunities to estimate are all over the place. Suppose you need to fill a container with raisins, put folded towels on a shelf, or fill a bowl with apples. Ask your child to estimate how many will fit before it's actually done and then count the actual number after. How many steps is it from the living room to the bathroom? How many jellybeans will fit in the jar? How many words are on a page?

Two by Two

To reinforce the concept of pairs and to learn to count by 2s, ask your child to help make a list of what comes in pairs. Do you know any twins? What about shoes, or socks, or earrings, or earmuffs? When the list is complete, help her count all the pairs by 2s. Another way to go about this is to buy a bag of peanuts and talk about how many nuts are in each shell. It's almost always a pair. Count each peanut with your child by 2s and then open them and see how many pairs there really were by lining the nuts up in rows of pairs. Is there one left?

6 & UP

SKILLS

✓ Counting

✓ Sets and Groups

Secret Codes

Children like the mystery of writing by codes. You or your child write out all the letters in the alphabet on a sheet of paper. Leave enough room underneath each letter to write numbers 1 through 26 ("a" being 1, "z" being 26). This is good practice and requires good concentration skills.

Practice encoding some messages using numbers instead of the letters by referring to the code chart. Your child might need help from another person to write down her message without your seeing it first. Then she can encode the message herself by looking at the chart and then ask you to decode it. Or, your child and a friend might leave messages for each other using this code. What about using it to leave simple messages for the family on the refrigerator? And of course you might always use higher numbers—starting at 20 for "a," for example.

Basic Shapes

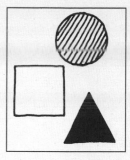

To reinforce geometric shapes, draw a curvy snakelike solid shape on a big piece of construction paper to make a game board. Make one end the place to "start" and the other the goal (maybe your child can draw a brick school made out of rectangular bricks). Divide this curve into small, equal segments and in each segment draw a square, a triangle, a circle, and a rectangle. For more experienced players, you could use solid geometrical shapes, such as a rhombus, a cone, or a cube. Then draw these shapes again on a piece of paper and make copies so that when you cut the shapes apart you'll have about fifteen of each shape. Gather some markers together, such as pennies or Lego pieces. To play, place these shapes face down in a pile and one child at a time picks the top card and places a marker on the first matching shape on the board. When the game gets going and you draw a card whose matching shapes are covered, you miss that turn. Make sure you mention the shape names as you play along, but don't belabor it.

5 & UP

SKILLS

✓ Geometric shapes

✓ Visual discrimination

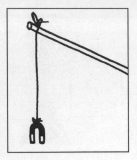

Fish for Equations

SKILLS

✓ Sets and groups
✓ Problem solving

To compute simple (or not so simple) equations, it's fun to fish for them! Get some dowels at the hardware store and at the end of each tie a small magnet. (Small magnets can be bought in hardware or craft stores.) Then place in a box some cards with a number written on each and a paper clip attached to every card. Players should not be able to see the cards they're fishing for. You can start with each player fishing out two cards and adding them together, or you can progress to three or four cards at a time. For younger children, it would be helpful to color in the appropriate number of dots on each end for a visual aid. Of course, you could use subtraction and multiplication operations as well in this game.

Stop!

Check out the shapes of road signs as you travel around. The most familiar is probably the STOP sign and this is an opportunity to explain that its shape is an octagon. Other signs bring up more new vocabulary—the school crossing sign is a pentagon. Explain to your child that these words reveal the number of sides the shape has. Begin a collection of various road signs. Help your child draw some. Eventually you and your child can sort them and try to determine if there's any pattern. For example, are there any other octagon signs, or what kinds of signs are triangular?

SKILLS

✓ **Geometric shapes**

✓ **Language acquisition**

✓ **Observation**

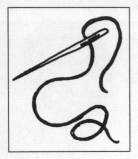

Parabolas

SKILLS

✓ Geometric shapes

✓ Eye/hand coordination

On a piece of oaktag about 6" by 6" or larger, mark off 11 half-inch segments along the left side and 11 half-inch segments along the bottom. Then on the left side write the numbers 1 through 10 from top to bottom, leaving the last ½ inch free. Along the bottom leave the first segment free also and write the numbers 1 through 10 across from left to right. This leaves the left corner of the graph blank. Next to each number make a hold with a plastic sewing needle. When all the holes are in place, thread the needle with bright embroidery yarn and ask your child to sew up from the bottom of "1" and down through the hole of the other number "1." Continue this from "2" to "2" and so on. The end result is a parabola and an attractive design as well. You could use a different color thread for each number sequence for even more effect.

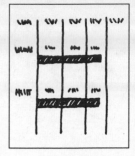

Growing Up

Make a graph to observe your child's growth pattern. As in all graphs, this one will make it much easier to see the changes in height and weight as the months go by. You could do it monthly, but the changes might be very subtle. Try instead to use various milestones as times to record the information. Maybe family birthdays, and holidays, or seasons might be just enough apart so that the data are more striking.

On a big piece of paper write either the months or the milestones across the top then on the left side write "weight" and "height" under it. Fill in the numbers at the appropriate time and watch the numbers get larger!

3 & UP

SKILLS

✓ Measurement

✓ Making comparisons

Silent Math

To practice working with equations, try acting them out. Write different equations on separate cards. Turn one over, for example: $5 - 5 = ?$ and ask your child to illustrate the equation using materials that are handy. Or, if you have a few children, one child at a time could turn over a card, not show it to the others, and demonstrate the problem for the others to guess which equation it is. It's tricky for children to conceptualize a math equation without talking, using only objects. And to guess the answer can be even harder.

Roman Numerals

Roman numerals are letters that represent numbers. For a child who knows the alphabet and numbers up to 30 or more, these numerals are fascinating to learn. A good idea is to make a chart of them and write the roman numeral on top of the number it represents. Demonstrate the way addition and subtraction are used, but don't expect that your child will automatically pick it up—this is a whole new system of numbers! Linking up roman numerals to your child's own world makes sense and a good place to start is with some chapter books. *Charlotte's Web* by E. B. White is a wonderful example because you can read the chapters as well! Of course, looking around for other places where roman numerals are used is an interesting hunt but it might prove a bit daunting for your child (or you) to have to translate the letters into numbers. Sometimes just noticing them is enough, but do write them down and decipher them together when you get home.

SKILLS

✓ Observation

✓ Numeral recognition

Shopping for Shapes

5 & UP

Take a trip to the supermarket to look for shapes. Make sure you take some paper (and maybe a clipboard) to note everything down. When you get home, go over the list with your child and discuss what you both found. Your child can copy the name of the item, for example, an orange, and draw an illustration next to it. Then, as a further activity, you could help him sort and classify all the different shapes by cutting them out. Asking some leading questions can be helpful while in the store, especially if your child is young. Supermarkets can be a little overwhelming! Suggest looking for bread shapes, or crackers, from the illustration on the box. What about fruits and vegetables? Try to keep a loose idea of what the shape can be, for example: toilet paper is a circle, especially at one end; tomatoes are circles, or spheres if your child is a bit older. What about different shapes of bottles? After everything's sorted out, decide which shape showed up most.

Keeping Track

Depending on the age of your child, do some counting activities around your daily routines. How many steps do we climb in a day? How many blocks do we walk? How far is it (how many steps) from the bathroom to the kitchen? How many steps to the nearest store? How many steps across is the living room? Record some of this information after two or three different people have counted their own steps. Discuss with your child any differences you find, such as she walks twenty-five steps from the front door to the kitchen while Dad does it in seventeen steps.

5 & UP

SKILLS

✓ Counting

✓ Making comparisons

✓ Observation

SKILLS

✓ **Measurement**

✓ **Making comparisons**

Light and Heavy

Save some plastic containers of the same size, such as plastic soda bottles or quart juice containers. Then fill each container (maybe six in total) with a different amount of dirt, sand, pebbles, or rice. Ask your child to pick each of them up and talk together about how light or heavy it seems. Then ask her if she can arrange them in order of the lightest to the heaviest. Help her go through the group one at a time, looking for the next size. Obviously, if you have too many containers it will be hard to discern the weight difference of each, so it's best to start with very clear gradations. This way a younger child can clearly feel the differences and will be able to order them herself after a while. This activity could be expanded for an older child by using different kinds of containers in larger numbers.

Keeping Time

"Why do you think we need to know what time it is and why do we use clocks?" Consider these questions with your child and write down his answers. The sun might help us in some basic ways, but how would he know when to take his medicine? And what about the movie schedule? And think about the time you missed the plane. Think about all the places where we see clocks—by the side of the bed, in the classroom, on people's wrists, at train stations. Make a list of other places where clocks are important.

SKILLS

✓ Time

✓ Observation

✓ Collecting and recording data

SKILLS

✓ Time

Beginning Time

Telling time on standard clocks is difficult for a young child. To help recognize what various times look like on a clock, give your child either an old clock that doesn't work or make a cardboard one. If she wants to know when Grandma is coming, set the old clock to 3:30 and tell her that when the clock in the kitchen matches that time, Grandma will be arriving. Do this whenever the subject of time comes up to familiarize her with the concepts of telling time and using clocks.

Time Problems

Use an old clock for this activity, or make a cardboard one. Place the hands on 12 o'clock. Then ask your child, "What time it will be in 2 hours? 4 hours? 6 hours?" Ask him to move the hands to indicate the new time. You can also work backward. Ask him to show you what time was it one hour ago? Three hours ago? Twelve hours ago? If he's mastered the hours, try the half ones. For example, move the hands so that they will show what time it will be 1½ hours from now.

5 & UP

SKILLS

✓ Time

✓ Counting

SKILLS

✓ Time

✓ Counting

Kitchen Time

Experiment with the kitchen timer to demonstrate how long minutes are. Suppose you'll be ready to go shopping in fifteen minutes. Demonstrate that each notch on the timer is a minute, and then help her count fifteen of them and turn the dial. When it rings, it will be time to go. Use the timer like this to measure small amounts of time on a continuous basis to help your child get a better feel for minutes passing by. She can set it herself when she needs to know when to stop doing something; for example, if she's tempted to dawdle in the tub and then miss her bedtime story, she can bring the timer with her into the bathroom.

How Long Is a Minute?

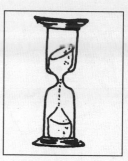

Your child will understand just how long a minute is if it's directly related to his own experience. Play these games with him for about the length of a minute. How many times does he think he can write his name in a minute? How about jump on one foot? Say a nursery rhyme? When he's estimated the number, then he can actually do it and see not only how close he gets, but also how long or short a minute is when he's doing familiar activities.

5 & UP

SKILLS

✓ Time

✓ Counting

✓ Estimation

Number Sentence Challenge

SKILLS

✓ Sets and groups

✓ Problem solving

This could be a good game for three or four children, and it provides practice computing equations or number sentences. Somebody starts with a number sentence; for example, 2 + 3 = 5. Then the next person makes up a number sentence that begins with the answer to the previous one: for example, 5 + 1 = 6. The next person's equation begins with 6, and so on. Obviously, if you're playing this as a game, as the numbers go up, the problems are more sophisticated. If they've reached their limit, the players can begin again with one and use different equations. It's a good idea to have a box of some sort of counters nearby (beans, buttons, pennies, etc.), so your child can use them in solving the equations.

Weaving

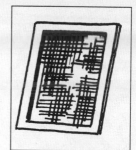

Weaving things both helps develop small motor skills and offers an opportunity to create patterns. You can use an old picture frame and attach rug mesh across it with tacks. The rug mesh can be bought in a crafts store, and so can the macramé thread that you use to weave with. Cut the macramé thread into strips a couple of inches longer than the frame and knot one end of each piece. Then fasten some tape on the other end to make a point, like a shoelace. Ask your child to place one hand under the frame and with the other hand insert the taped end through the mesh up and down all the way across. Repeat this with each piece of macramé thread. For a younger child, just the weaving experience will be satisfying enough, without bothering with a particular pattern. For an older child, ask about her ideas for a pattern and buy these particular colors. Perhaps drawing the pattern first on a piece of paper with markers would be a good idea, so she can work from a model.

5 & UP

SKILLS

✓ Patterns

✓ Eye/hand coordination

✓ Small motor development

All-Weather Weaving

SKILLS

✓ Patterns

✓ Eye/hand
coordination

✓ Imaginative
thinking

For a really unique experience of weaving, do it outside! Maybe the wall of the garage will do, or a section of wooden fence. Whichever place you choose, all you need to do is hammer some nails along the top and bottom of the area every foot or so. The nails on top must be directly opposite the bottom ones, so that you can loop some strong string around each pair to make the warp to weave through. For weaving across, you can use all kinds of materials—remember you're outside. How about leaves, or an occasional flower with its stem, or bits of grass tied together? Talk about possible materials first, but as the weaving evolves, you might just use what strikes you at the moment.

Nature Weaving

For a small version of "nature weaving," look around with your child for a forked branch 1 foot or 2 long. Get a long piece of yarn or string and wrap it around the two forks, so that you make a warp to weave through. Don't worry if it's uneven, this is supposed to look "natural." Then look around with your child for small weaving materials, such as clover, a dandelion, leaves, or grass. You can also use bits of string or ribbon, but the idea is to create a weaving that represents the many different natural ingredients found outside your house. These weavings look great hanging on a wall inside your house for decoration.

5 & UP

SKILLS

✓ Patterns

✓ Eye/hand coordination

✓ Imaginative thinking

Grocery Bargains

SKILLS

✓ Money

✓ Problem solving

If your child is learning about money either in school or at home, this activity can be good practice as well as useful to the family! Get the latest circular announcing sales from the supermarket and tell your child that she has a certain amount of money, for example $5.00, to spend for items on the list. Determine a range of choices, such as fruits and vegetables, or cleaning products. Then help your child prepare a grocery list that comes close to the amount of money specified. Supply lots of paper and pencil for doing the addition, and maybe a calculator, as well. Learning how to use a calculator as a tool in math operations can be useful for children of all ages. Your child can then combine pencil-and-paper math, doing operations in her head, and maybe using counters along with the calculator, thereby experiencing all the different ways math can be done in the real world!

Counting Stamps

This is a good activity for holiday time, but if you're simply out of stamps you can do it, too. Tell your child you need to go to the post office to buy some stamps. They come in packs of 10, and they cost 33 cents each. Suppose you need to buy 15 stamps, or 20, or 35. Ask your child to calculate how much money you will need to spend for a specific amount. This task can be particularly engrossing if your child needs to send out birthday party invitations. Talk about different ways to find the right amount of money. You can count by 10s, but what do you do with those 2s? Could you count by 2s as well? Get out a pencil and paper and try out various methods. Maybe drawing all the stamps first is a good idea, so you can see what 25 or 30 looks like, or maybe just doing the calculator is enough. "How could you use the calculator to help with this problem?"

6 & UP

SKILLS

✓ Money

✓ Problem solving

✓ Counting

It's Laundry Time!

3 & UP

For younger children especially, it's an interesting task to sort the laundry, either dirty or clean. Suppose it's dirty and you ask your child to think about what needs to be washed. Write down what he says and maybe draw a quick picture next to the word. If he only thinks of jeans and socks, remind him about other clothes we wear and also about towels, sheets, and so on. Ask him how many items he thinks there will be. After the list is finished, get out the dirty laundry and sort it with your child. When it's sorted, see how it matches the list. Were there really ten towels, or one hundred socks?

A Hundred Is . . .

Understanding what 100 is can be a difficult concept for young children. They might be able to count to 100, either by 1's or 10's or even 2's and 5's. But do they really know what 100 looks like? Talk about 100 with your child and suggest that she make some collections of 100 things. Suppose you put 100 rubber bands in a container. What would it look like? What about 100 bottle caps, or 100 dimes, or 100 pennies, or 100 small toys of any kind? Actually doing 100 and seeing 100 helps a child comprehend what 100 really is.

6 & UP

SKILLS

✓ Estimating

✓ Counting

✓ Problem solving

Coin Exchange

When children have begun to understand the value of coins up to 25 cents or a quarter, you can make a game out of exchanging smaller coins for larger ones. Make a spinner divided into three sections with the numbers 1, 2, and 3 written in each section. For each child playing, there should be ten pennies, ten nickels, and two quarters. Put them in a dish in the middle and put in a few extra pennies and nickels, as well. When the player spins a number, she picks up that many pennies. The object is to exchange the pennies for a nickel when she has five and then eventually be able to exchange five nickels for a quarter.

Money Problems

When your child has begun to work with money in math, this is a good activity for reinforcement. Give your child three pennies and four dimes, and ask her to solve these problems with them: "I have 4 coins worth 40 cents"; "I have 4 coins worth 22 cents"; "I have 3 coins worth 13 cents"; "I have 4 coins worth 31 cents." You can do this activity with any combination of coins, and it's really much more meaningful to have actual coins to work with. Perhaps your child might like to pick two or more coins and make up some problems on her own. Then she can test them out on a sibling or a friend.

6 & UP

SKILLS

✓ Money

✓ Problem solving

Adding Coins

SKILLS

✓ Money

✓ Problem solving

Solve number sentences, or equations, by using coins only. Write down the equations on cards and get a collection of pennies and nickels for younger children, and dimes and quarters for older children. Hold up a card and ask your child to solve the equation using coins. It might help to make a chart to help your child visualize the value of individual coins. You could glue each particular coin and then write its value next to it. The hardest part, however, is calculating the amount. If you use only pennies, nickels, and dimes, your child can count by ones, fives, and tens using the coins. But when you combine coins or just move up to larger numbers, the calculator might come in handy. For example, for an older child, if you have the equation $35 + 45 =$, it might be enough of a challenge for him to separate out the coins to use to solve it, such a dimes, nickels, or quarters, and the actual answer would be necessary but secondary.

Guess My Coin!

Talk about the attributes of a penny, a nickel, a dime, and a quarter. "The penny is copper colored, it's bigger than a dime, it has Abraham Lincoln on it." "A dime is the smallest, it is silver plated, it also has man on it." Ask your child to describe the coins and ask questions about what she notices. "How are a penny and a dime different?" Then play this game. Your child puts a coin in her hand and hides both hands. You need to guess which hand. If you guess correctly, you need to identify the coin. Then you hide a coin and ask your child to name it. You get another guess if you miss the first time.

6 & UP

SKILLS

✓ **Money**

✓ **Observation**

187

Un, Deux, Trois

SKILLS

✓ Counting

✓ Language acquisition

✓ Sight word recognition

Teach your child to count to 10 in another language. If you or someone in your family know another language, begin with that. Make a set of cards with English number words on them and then another set with number words from another language. Figure out with your child whom you know that speaks a foreign language and ask them to teach you how to count in their language. Mostly, children learn by the sounds of words, but if your child is beginning to read, it's a good idea to write the words on separate cards. Make sure you also write the numeral on each one. "Un, deux, trois, quatre, cinque, six, sept, huit, neuf, dix!"

Counting by Tens

To practice counting by 10's and grouping by 10's, count out 100 beans, but don't let your child know how many there are. Get 10 paper cups or yogurt containers and ask your child to count out 10 beans for each cup. Explain that if she counts by 10's, she can find out how many beans there are altogether. Let her try it. Then, suppose you moved five cups aside—how many beans are in the remaining cups? Maybe your child will want to group the cups in different ways and continue to count by 10's to see how many beans there are. This kind of hands-on activity helps create a clearer picture of what grouping by 10's and counting by 10's is all about.

6 & UP

SKILLS

✓ Counting

✓ Sets and groups

Bean Sticks

If your child is learning place value in school, this is a good activity to complement it. Get ten or more tongue depressors and a bag of small beans. Ask your child to count out ten beans and glue them onto each tongue depressor (it's a tedious chore to glue all the beans, so you can help, as well). Explain that this is a "ten stick" and that you can count by 10's with them and can also use it to discover how many sets of ten there are in a large number. For example: how could you make the number 30 using the ten sticks? Answer: you'd have three sets of ten, or three sticks. Practice different numbers with your child and help her sort the ten sticks to represent each number. But remember, it's a difficult concept for even a first-grade child to grasp that each stick is really a 10, not a 1. To help with this, have a pile of loose beans available and practice counting with the ten sticks and the loose beans. Ask her to make the number 17 by using both the ten sticks and the loose beans. This concept takes time to fully internalize.

Cardboard Calculator

Find a small cardboard box with a cover. Keep the cover on and cut two holes in it. On the side of the box near the bottom cut another hole. Have a set of cards with number sentences written on them, but with no answers. Turn over a card and have your child drop the appropriate number of beans into the top holes. For example, if the problem is 5 + 3 = . . . , she should put 5 beans in one hole and 3 beans in the other. Then ask her to do the problem, and then check her answer by tipping the box so that the beans fall out and she then can count them.

SKILLS

✓ Sets and groups

✓ Counting

✓ Problem solving

100 Bingo

"**1**00 Bingo" can be played on a homemade board that you have designed with the numbers 1 to 100 arranged in rows of ten. Make a set of number cards for 1 to 100. The first player picks a card from the pile and covers that number on the 100 board with a counter of some kind (a coin, a tile, uncooked pasta). Put the card in a separate pile. Continue playing until one player has 5 counters in a row, either horizontally, vertically, or on a diagonal. For older children and a more challenging game, the player adds or subtracts any given number, for example, a 3 from the number on the card, and places her counter on that number on the board.

Bean Equations

Get an egg carton and write the numbers 1 to 12 in the cups. Your child can play alone or it can be a game with other players. Each person puts two beans or other light objects inside the carton, closes the lid and shakes the carton. When the carton is opened the child needs to write (or do in her head) a number sentence based on the numbers where the beans have landed. Then, by counting some objects or in her head, she has to come up with the answer.

SKILLS

✓ Problem solving

✓ Sets and groups

SKILLS

✓ **Sorting and classifying**

✓ **Problem solving**

✓ **Critical thinking**

Venn Diagrams

Venn diagrams are circles with labels put inside them to indicate what should go in each circle. For example, a circle could say, "I am wearing blue," and another circle could say, "I am wearing yellow." Then whoever is in the room could write their name on a piece of paper and put it in the appropriate circle. But what if you're wearing both blue and yellow? Then the two circles should overlap or intersect so that the third section is made for those that are wearing both colors. Venn diagrams are used to sort and classify and can be very simple, such as, "I am wearing red," or more complicated, containing a number of different characteristics. You can draw them on paper or make circles out of yarn and place them on a table. If there is an intersection, the two circles are moved toward each other so that they overlap in the center. Think about some characteristics about people in your house that you can use to make a Venn diagram. Some people won't fit the categories at all, and they can write their name on paper and place it outside the circle.

Catalog Shopping

For older children who can handle larger sums of money, use some old catalogs to "shop" from at home. Pick an amount of money that makes sense for the particular type of catalog and ask your child to make a list of items that she would like that amounts as closely as possible to the number given. Suppose your child had $50.00 to spend in a pet catalog or $100.00 in a clothes catalog. See if you can work together to reach the amount using pencil and paper for one amount and the calculator for another.

6 & UP

SKILLS
✓ Money
✓ Problem solving

Number Patterns

SKILLS

✓ Patterns

✓ Numeral
recognition

Draw a 100's chart with ten rows of ten numbers. Ask your child to cover all the numbers that have 2 in them. You can cover the numbers with a temporary marker, such as a penny, or color each space with a light-colored crayon. Make up other directions, such as covering all the numbers with zero in them, numbers that have a circle, or numbers where both digits are the same. The point is to notice patterns on the number chart. Some are especially clear, like the zero numbers, and others require a little more thought. But all of these show important relationships between numbers.

You've Got a Temperature!

Measuring temperatures is an interesting activity for both younger and older children. For the older ones, it's helpful to compare the temperature readings from both a Celsius and Fahrenheit thermometer. Children could also look in the newspaper and make a note about the daily temperature in your area and make some kind of a chart showing the fluctuations. You could draw the thermometer, draw lines for each temperature, and write the date. Or you could compare the newspaper's account with the reading on your own thermometer. Or place a thermometer in a bowl of water and record the temperature. Then put some ice cubes in the water and check again. These activities help both create a basic understanding about cold and hot temperatures and familiarize your child with thermometers.

SKILLS

✓ Measurement

✓ Experimenting

✓ Drawing conclusions

SKILLS

✓ Money

✓ Observation

Coins Only!

Check out places where you pay for things in coins, like a public telephone, a toll booth, or a vending machine that sells candy and chips. Ask your child to think of other places where coins are deposited. What about the Laundromat or even the various machines in an amusement park that use only coins? Figure out together which machines your family uses the most, and next time you have the chance, ask your child to select the coins to pay for the toll, or the fortune telling machine, or the soda she wants.

Recycling Math

Recycling soda cans and bottles doesn't just improve the environment, it can provide a good math experience as well. If each empty can is worth 5 cents, this is a perfect opportunity to count by 5's with your child. Look at the recycling bin when you're in the store or at home and ask your child to estimate how many cans and bottles it contains. Then, maybe with the help of a pencil and paper, figure out together how much of a refund someone would get for all those cans.

SKILLS

✓ Counting

✓ Money

✓ Estimation

SKILLS

✓ **Counting**

✓ **Money**

✓ **Problem solving**

Bank on It

Opening a bank account for your child is a very direct way for him to experience the world of checks and passbooks, tellers, and safety deposit boxes. Obviously, you need to begin with some money. Maybe this could be an accumulation of allowance money, birthday money, or maybe some "seed" money from you. Take a trip to the bank and go through the process of opening a savings account together. Explain how the account works, including the fact that the bank will give him extra money to add to his own savings. All of this should be geared to the age of your child, of course. The word *interest* doesn't need to be explained in percentages as long as the idea is talked about. Part of this procedure might include an idea for using the savings eventually. If a new bike or computer is the goal, it makes it all less abstract. But planning to buy something shouldn't be the whole point. Saving money should be an ongoing habit, and it's a good lesson to start young.

Cutting Coupons

If your child can help you figure out bargains from grocery circulars, she might have a go at coupons. Get into the habit of looking at them in the newspapers with your child. Ask her to cut out ones that both of you think you could use. Start with familiar items. Then take a trip to the supermarket with some coupons. Find a particular item and see how much you'll save with the coupon. A calculator might come in handy, but maybe your child can do it in her head. Maybe the savings could go into a special jar at home and when the amount reaches $10.00, it could be deposited in your child's savings account.

SKILLS

✓ **Money**

✓ **Problem solving**

Opening a Restaurant

SKILLS

✓ **Money**

✓ **Imaginative thinking**

✓ **Drawing and painting**

✓ **Sight word recognition**

How about opening a restaurant in your home? There are two ways to go about this, but both have the same goal, to have fun and help your child do some math. It's up to you to steer this in the right direction so that the money involved suits your child's capabilities. For younger children, make some reusable food from paper mâché. Just make a flour and water mixture that is a little thicker than pancake batter and dip various strips of newspaper into it to fashion things like hamburgers, vegetables, or ice cream. See how creative everyone can get! Paint all this when it's dry and you've got a movable feast. Then talk about a menu. Help write one that's simple and come up with some pieces that reflect the math level of your child, not reality. Maybe even pennies—for example a hamburger could cost 5 cents. Make an order pad for the Waiter to use and "go out to eat!"

Menu Math

You can also play restaurant with a real meal or snack. This might work better with an older child. Talk about prices of food that are more realistic and use actual money. Make a menu listing the foods being served and an order pad. Perhaps you'll deal with only round numbers, such as pasta will cost $5.00. Maybe you can use "mental math" to solve the total of the bill. Otherwise, if it's $5.25, a calculator might come in handy. Cook the food together and enjoy your meal!

SKILLS

✓ Money

✓ Sight word recognition

✓ Problem solving

Coin Rubbings

SKILLS

✓ Money

✓ Eye/hand coordination

A helpful activity to do when your child is beginning to recognize coins is coin rubbings. Introduce one coin at a time. Ask your child to examine both sides of the coin and talk about the design. Remember to point out the year the coin was minted. Then put the coin under the sheet of white paper and rub over it with a crayon. Sometimes it helps to use the broadside of the crayon, without the paper, to do the rubbing. Make rubbings of both sides. This activity helps familiarize your child with coins.

Number Concentration

Younger children enjoy making their own Concentration game from old calendars. Find two old calendars; the bigger the better. Help your child cut out all the numbers and then sort them so that you have doubles of each one. The next step is to glue each on an index card. Your child might want to decorate the backs of each card, but the trick is to keep the design the same on every card so that they all look alike when you're playing. Maybe stickers on each would be a good idea. The point of the game is to find matches by remembering the location of the numbers, so drawing on the backs might be a giveaway. But it's your child's game, so let him decide.

5 & UP

SKILLS

✓ Numeral recognition

✓ Drawing and painting

✓ Visual discrimination

Cook with Patterns

SKILLS

✓ Patterns

A great way to extend working with patterns is to cook with them. If you're grilling any food on skewers, it's a wonderful opportunity to ask your child to help create the patterns. What about one piece of pineapple and one piece of chicken? Or, one pineapple, one pepper, one chicken? Or, to make it harder, two green peppers, one chicken, two red peppers, one pineapple. This could go on forever, as patterns can, and it's a perfect way to help your child see how patterns exist in the real world.

Packing It Up

The next time you plan to go grocery shopping, talk to your child first about what kinds of food comes in packages of more than one item. She'll probably think of cans of soda or maybe packs of pudding, but does she know how many are in each package? When you get to the store, explore. See how many packs of things you can find. It's a good idea to bring a homemade clipboard with you, so that you can keep a list. This is a math lesson that zeros in on groups of things. As in dominoes, when your child looks at a pattern and automatically knows it's a 5 or a 6, here she will have a chance to get used to groups in packaging. "Are there any 12's or 18's?" The activity also offers an opportunity to count by 2's, 3's, or 6's.

5 & UP

SKILLS

✓ Sets and groups

✓ Problem solving

Weighing In

If your child is learning about pounds and ounces in school, asking her to weigh the produce you buy at the grocery store is a sure-fire activity, even if you wouldn't necessarily weigh it yourself. For a younger child, just using the scales and furthering her understanding of what weighing is all about is enough. Let her hold a bag of grapes to put in the scale. Then give her something lighter like a tomato and ask which she thinks is heavier. Then ask her which reached the biggest number on the scale. Of course, looking at the numbers on the scale helps with number recognition as well. Explain how the numbers work on the particular scale and make sure you don't omit saying that there are ¼ pounds, ½ pounds, and so forth. Even though your child might not understand fractions yet, there's no good reason not to let her know they exist. It will just continue to expand the process of discovering the many ways in which numbers are used.

100's Collage

To further experience what 100 looks like, gather 100 small objects with your child. They could all be the same, or you could have a mixture of objects relatively the same size, such as buttons, bottle caps, crayons, seeds, pebbles, watermelon seeds, or popsicle sticks. When you have counted out 100, glue them on construction paper for a colorful and mathematical collage. Before you glue them, this is a good opportunity to divide the objects into sets of 10, 2, or 5. Seeing that these smaller groups together add up to 100 helps your child visualize 100 in different ways. It's not necessary for your child to be able to count by 2's or 5's to form sets. Work backward; start with the 100 objects you've collected, then pick a number for the sets you want to make and then count them off together. Afterward, count the sets you've made, as well: "We've got 20 sets of 5 that equal 100"; or "We've got 33 sets of 3, with 1 set of 1." This all works best when you have a large surface to work on, such as the floor or a table so there is plenty of room to arrange the sets.

SKILLS

✓ Counting

✓ Estimation

✓ Imaginative thinking

✓ Sets and groups

At a Glance

Arranging things in groups or sets makes it easier for young children to visualize exactly what numbers are. To tell at a glance exactly what number a set represents, it helps to arrange the objects in an ordered form. For example, if you had twenty pennies thrown haphazardly on a table, it would be difficult to see how many pennies there were without counting each one. But if you can arrange the pennies in positions, your child can learn to tell quickly how many pennies there are. Suppose you put the pennies in groups of 2's, 4's, or 5's and arranged the sets in a straight line across the table. Can you see how much simpler it is to "know" the number? This is so particularly for larger numbers, and it helps your child recognize them without depending on counting.

Grouping

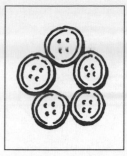

Take a number of objects—say twelve buttons. Put them out in a zigzag on a table and ask your child to look at them quickly and guess how many there are. He probably won't be able to guess correctly. Now arrange the buttons in groups of 3's and show just one group to your child and ask how many there are. Now uncover all four groups and ask how many in all. This should make it a lot easier to tell at a glance without counting. Practice arranging items in small groups and help your child get used to forming larger numbers this way.

Dice Math

SKILLS

✓ Counting

✓ Problem solving

To help your child become familiar with dot arrangements on dice, as well as practice doing addition, play this game. It helps to have three or four players. One person rolls the pair of dice. Whoever adds the numbers correctly first gets to roll the dice next. Dice are important tools in math, and it's particularly important for your child to memorize the arrangement of dots that represent the number because these conformations appear throughout math activities. Eventually, your child will "know" a 5 at a glance, and this will speed up using dice in games. It's always a good idea to have a collection of counters for children to use when adding two sets of numbers.

Flipping Coins

To work with the problem of probability, flip some coins. First make sure your child knows the "head" and "tail" of a penny. A few children should do the activity together so they can compare the outcomes. Give each child ten pennies and two sheets of paper with "Heads" written on one sheet and "Tails" on the other. Each child flips his or her penny and puts a tally mark on the appropriate sheet of paper. Finally, everyone checks out each other's papers and looks for similarities.

SKILLS

✓ Money

Odd or Even?

SKILLS

✓ Patterns

✓ Counting

✓ Problem solving

Even numbers can be divided by 2, odd numbers can't. Look at numbers up to 30 with an older child. Which is even, 1 or 2, 3 or 4? Help your child discern the pattern of odd and even numbers on a number line after you've worked together figuring out which numbers are the ones you can count by 2's and which numbers can't be counted that way. When she sees that every other number is either odd or even (depending on where you start), it will make more sense to her.

Odd/Even Sums

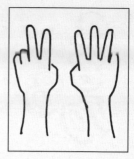

To help your child learn even and odd numbers play this game with a few people. You could even have teams if you've got three or four people for each team. Ask two people to stand with their backs to each other and hold up any number of fingers. The people watching then add the fingers of both players together and decide if the sum is even or odd. If you're using teams, one could be the odd team and the other the even one. Have someone record the scores and see which team has the most scores when you're done. Having a number line handy and some counters might be a good idea.

SKILLS

✓ **Problem solving**

SKILLS

✓ Patterns

✓ Counting

Chains of Numbers

Numbers series are chains of numbers that follow a certain pattern. For example, suppose you had 2, 4, 6, 8. How could you continue the pattern? There are an infinite number of patterns that you can create in a series. Suppose you had 1, 3, 5, or 10, 20, 30, 40. Or, 1,2,4,8. What's the pattern here? Brainstorm with your child and see if you can come up with some number series on your own. In devising your own, or simply continuing a given series, your child will build a better understanding of the relationships between numbers.

Science
Activities

Science depends on curiosity and asking questions. A child's observations can lead to a hypothesis such as "Plants need sunshine to survive." An experiment should then follow, to prove whether this hypothesis is accurate. Recording the experiment, by writing and drawing what you see, is a scientific method. Finally, a conclusion will be reached. It's important to remember that for young children, science is about observing and making comparisons, not long explanations. You don't need to go into the complete scientific underpinnings of every phenomenon.

A Rotten Log

Go for a walk with your child in the backyard or local park and find a large log or piece of wood that is decaying. (If you prepare in advance, you can "plant" a log with your child the year before.) Ask your child questions about it, such as "What do you think makes it decay?" or "What do you think will happen to it over time?" Create a log book and write down your child's responses. Decide on a hypothesis, such as "The log will disappear into the ground" or "The log will last forever." Then continue to watch the log and record what you see.

You can also observe what kind of life the log supports. Are there worms or larvae that live on it? How about insects? Who lives underneath it? Why do they like it there? This might lead you to the local library, bookstore, or science museum to do research on insects and the natural world. Always handle the log gently and carefully and teach your child to handle the creatures who live on it with respect.

SKILLS

✓ Asking questions

✓ Observation

✓ Collecting and recording data

✓ Drawing conclusions

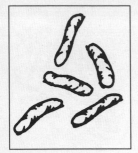

SKILLS

✓ **Asking questions**

✓ **Observation**

Mealworms

The life cycle of the mealworm provides an excellent framework for understanding a metamorphic insect. The life cycle, or metamorphosis, of most insects has four parts: the egg, the larva, the pupa, and the insect itself. Keeping mealworms at home sharpens the observational skills of children and introduces them to the difficult concept of the insect's development. An open plastic container with oatmeal and a slice of apple are all the insects need for their habitat, and children are free to investigate it on their own and observe the various stages (the eggs, however, are invisible). Mealworms can be bought in almost any pet store.

Mealworm Life Cycle

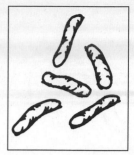

An extension of the life cycle activity is to provide a tray, so that the insects can be removed from the container and observed more closely. Magnifying glasses also come in handy. The mealworms in the larva stage of the beetle and the segments on their bodies are particularly clear under the magnifying glass. Encourage your child to notice how the mealworm moves, to see if she can tell the front end from the back. Are there any legs? What about antennae? The pupas and the beetles also can be examined closely, although it's a trick to keep the beetles on the tray, as well as fun! The fact that every kind of insect has six legs is reinforced when observing these beetles under the magnifying glass. These insect "pets" can be kept for years if the oatmeal is replenished and slices of apple or potato are provided for moisture. As with every living thing, care should be taken to handle the creatures gently and respectfully. Mealworms can be bought in almost any pet store. Don't worry about whether they will escape their home—they just remain in the oatmeal and go about their business.

3 & UP

Spiders!

SKILLS

✓ Observation

✓ Eye/hand coordination

Spiders can be kept in a terrarium with a screened cover. The habitat should have a soil-covered bottom, leaves and a rock or two. The ideal foods for them are live flies. They need a small bottle top full of water as well. Although catching flies can be fun (you might place some food on pieces of tape and hope to trap some) spider food (and spiders) can be ordered from Carolina Biological Company (see Resources).

With magnifying glasses, it is easy to observe that spiders have eight legs, thereby removing them from the insect world. They belong to the class Arachnida. What other characteristics do they have? What about wings or antennae? Nothing is as fascinating as a spider's web, especially the circular one of the orb weaver. And what better description of the building and the function of a web than the one in *Charlotte's Web* by E. B. White? This is a book that even young children love, and one chapter a night at bedtime can provide scientific information and literature at the same time.

Spider Webs

Children can build their own spider webs using black construction paper and white yarn or string. A good description of how a web is made can be found in a book called *Be Nice to Spiders* by Margaret Bloy Graham, which has a visual depiction of how it's all done. Start with a point in the center and glue pieces of strings from the center outward to about one inch from the edge of the paper. They should resemble spokes in a wheel. Then take longer string and circle it around the "web" a few times until you have a web that looks authentic. These webs are attractive in themselves, but they also can be used to make web prints by covering them in paint and transferring them onto paper.

3 & UP

SKILLS

✓ Observation

✓ Eye/hand coordination

Create a Spider

Replicas of spiders can be made out of two sections, or cups, of an egg carton, and some paint and pipe cleaners for legs. Talk about the anatomy of the spider with your child. How many body sections does it have and how many legs? Then proceed with your paper spider. Make sure the egg sections haven't been separated as these will represent the body. Help your child figure out how many legs go on each side and staple them in place. You can look at pictures of spiders and notice how the legs are bent and then make your spider leg's resemble them. Then your child can paint the whole thing. Again, it's a good idea to check out different types of spiders in books—then, the paint doesn't have to be just black.

Minibeast Logs

Observing and learning about different small creatures (or minibeasts) can lead to all kinds of writing activities. Certainly, if creatures are kept for any length of time, it is instructive to keep logs of your observations. Children can make their own logs by stapling sheets of paper together and writing the date for each observation. For example, a child might draw what he sees under a magnifying glass, such as the segments of a mealworm or a spider at rest in its web. He might also record any changes in the creature's environment, such as dead insects in the web or how much apple has disappeared over a week's time in the mealworm's habitat. You could also estimate or even count how many beetles or mealworms there are in the container at one time and then compare the amount a few weeks later. In this way, children hone their observational skills. Cycles in nature become more meaningful when children observe and record what they see and began to understand the continuation of generation after generation. When children directly experience these transformations in creatures' lives they acquire an intellectual concept that can be extended to many other situations.

5 & UP

SKILLS

✓ Observation

✓ Collecting and recording data

✓ Estimation

✓ Counting

Minibeast Riddles

SKILLS

✓ Critical thinking

✓ Observation

✓ Collecting and reading data

✓ Sight word recognition

✓ Drawing and painting

A writing activity related to learning about small creatures or minibeasts is to create riddles about them. Cut out a strip of construction paper 3" x 6". Onto it staple side by side two sections of small pieces of white paper with maybe five or six pieces in each section. In the first page help your child write clues about the minibeast she's thinking about. For example, "I have 8 legs," "I spin webs," and "I eat flies." Then flip up that page and reveal a picture your child has drawn of the creature. Leave room at the bottom for the simple sentence, "I am a spider." Continue on until both sections are filled up with riddles and answers. You could also staple paper in regular book fashion and write the riddle on the first page and the answer on the next or make individual riddle cards, with the clue on one side and the answer on the other.

Introducing the Slug

O f all the outside minibeast creatures to hunt for, the most prolific one you may find is the slug. Slugs hold a special fascination for children, probably because of their grotesque appearance, their size, and the ease with which they can be handled. Find some books at the library about slugs and discuss their attributes with your child—how their slime both helps propel them and serves as a deterrent to enemies (it tastes foul); where its nose is located; what it eats (mainly green plants); how it's both helpful and a nuisance to people; and the surprising fact that fireflies eat them. Then go out and lift some rocks or rotting logs in damp places and find your slugs. Scoop them up and put them in a terrarium filled with soil, rocks, and plants. Make sure you keep the soil damp at all times. There is one caveat about these creatures: their slime sticks incredibly to human hands. Scouring powder is the best way to remove it. Therefore, wearing plastic gloves is not such a bad idea!

5 & UP

SKILLS

✓ Observation

✓ Asking questions

✓ Drawing conclusions

225

Slug Math

SKILLS

✓ **Observation**

✓ **Collecting and recording data**

✓ **Measurement**

Several math activities can be done with slugs. Measuring them is a challenging one. Take a slug out of the terrarium (or if there are a few slugs and a few children, have each child choose a slug). Put the slug on a tray and find something you can measure it with. The best is a centimeter ruler, but a few small paperclips or strips of paper will also do. Children will discover that measuring a slug takes quite a while. Over time the slug keeps extending itself. When the child decides that the slug has reached its greatest length, he can record its length in a "slug log." Obviously, if more than one slug is being measured, the results can be compared.

Weighing a Slug

Activities that involve weighing slugs are of great interest to children and help provide early lessons in comparing weight. It's fun to use different kinds of scales. For a simple balance scale, put some buttons, beans, or pennies in one pan and a slug in the other. Your child could estimate first how many beans she thinks the slug might weigh and then experiment. She could keep a "slug log" with records of individual slugs' weight. For example, the smallest slug weighs five red buttons on June 26 and the largest one weighs eight red buttons on the same day. With careful observation, individual slugs can be recognized over time and their weight compared every few weeks or so.

5 & UP

SKILLS

✓ **Experimenting**

✓ **Collecting and recording data**

✓ **Measurement**

✓ **Making comparisons**

Slug Races

A very popular activity is a slug race. You need at least two slugs, but the more the merrier! Food, such as greens, fruit slices, or other vegetation can be placed at one end of a tray and the slugs placed at the other end. Children can use a timer that ticks off seconds to determine the winner. This is also a way to test food preference. A slice of onion, some bread, and some decaying or some fresh vegetables can be put on the tray and the child can record which food the slug prefers.

It is also possible to chart and test the steepest slope a slug can climb by placing a small board at graduated elevations. The rise of the slope can be measured underneath with small cubes or blocks and the information recorded in the "slug log."

Busy Bees

When reading books about bees, discuss with your child how they can not only hurt, but also help people. Most children know that they give us honey, but they might not know how bees help pollinate plants. Perhaps the best way to "explain" this to young children is to spend time in a garden observing bees. You can zero in on bees collecting nectar from flowers right under your nose. Point out that the fuzziness of the bee's body is fuzzy for a reason. In order for fruit to form, or more flowers to grow, it's necessary for the pollen (which is the male part of the plant) to reach the female part. The pollen sticks easily to the bee's fuzzy body and travels from one part of the plant to the other as the bee goes about collecting nectar for itself. Without the help of bees, most of the plants we know would not exist.

SKILLS

✓ Asking questions
✓ Observation

229

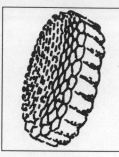

SKILLS

✓ **Observation**

✓ **Geometric shapes**

✓ **Eye/hand coordination**

Honeycombs

The subject of honey is an important part of the study of bees. Using a book as a reference, you can talk about the honeycomb, where the eggs are laid inside the hive. But going to a health food store and buying a piece of honeycomb is even better. Of course, if you can find an old unused hive, you might be lucky enough to find an old honeycomb. Talk about the shape of the cells in a honeycomb. Ask your child to count the sides, and if you have pattern blocks around, ask your child to find the one that matches. Pattern blocks are in every school, so your child can take a piece of honeycomb to school and pick out the corresponding block and share it with the class. Making your own replica of a honeycomb can be done by building one out of hexagon pattern blocks. Without the blocks, you might draw or cut a hexagon out of sturdy paper and your child can trace more of them to cut out. Then they can be used to fit together, just as the parts of a real honeycomb do.

Sweet as Honey

Agood extension of learning about bees and honey is to eat some honey. In a store, particularly a health food store, examine the different kinds of honey. Explain to your child that the names reflect the flowers the bees were sipping nectar from. Buy two or three kinds and have a tasting when you go home.

A good recipe using any kind of honey is for honeyballs. Pour out a cup or so of oatmeal on a baking sheet or tray and mix it up with a can of grated coconut. Then dribble some honey over it all and help your child roll it around and make balls. Refrigerate the balls briefly and enjoy!

SKILLS

✓ **Observation**

✓ **Small motor development**

Miniature Gardens

SKILLS

✓ Observation

✓ Collecting and recording data

✓ Imaginative thinking

✓ Drawing and painting

A colorful diorama can be created of a garden, complete with flowers and bees. A shoe box is the usual choice, but any box will do. Ask your child to paint the box and then when it's dry, help her decide how to make the garden and the insects. Cutting out pictures of flowers and gluing them to the back of the box is a good beginning. Making flowers for the foreground out of pipe cleaners and construction paper would work. Tissue paper, cellophane, colored tissues, or toilet paper can be cut up or bunched together to make flowers. Bees and other insects can be drawn and cut out of construction paper, or maybe some yellow and black yarn could be wrapped around in little balls to resemble bees. The final touch could be a cutout of a child in the midst of it all.

Minibeast Terrarium

You can introduce other minibeasts to the terrarium your child is keeping. Along with slugs and spiders, you can look for other beetles, ants, or centipedes outside and include them as well. From a nursery or garden catalog you can order ladybugs, but the Carolina Biological Catalog (see Resources) contains other insects as well. Particularly appealing are the butterfly pupas, which should be kept separately in their own containers until they hatch. Then they should be released outside. All of these ordered insects come with complete instructions and food. Caring for these creatures, watching them, handling them when possible, drawing them, and writing about them are all part of an exciting learning experience.

5 & UP

SKILLS

✓ Observation

✓ Collecting and recording data

✓ Drawing conclusions

Balloon Creatures

You can make papier-mâché models of various minibeasts. You need balloons of different sizes and shapes, paint, and pipe cleaners. To make papier-mâché you need some flour, water, and newspapers ripped into strips. Blow up the balloons to match the various body parts of the minibeast you've chosen. Tape together the appropriate number of balloons. Then make a mixture of flour and water and dip one strip of newspaper at a time into the mixture and then press each strip onto a balloon. Remember to run each strip between two fingers to get rid of the excess goo. Smooth the paper as carefully as you can on the balloons so that there won't be any edges or gaps when it's dry. After a day or so, attach pipe cleaner legs and wings with tape and then paint the model.

Minibeast Prints

W onderful prints that are suitable for greeting cards, calendars, or for frames can be made of minibeast drawings. What you need are pieces of styrofoam, such as the kind that meat or other groceries are wrapped in. Cut off the edges, so you have a flat piece of styrofoam. For the best result you should buy a brayer, a small roller that you use to press the print on paper. These come from art supply stores. The most effective prints are often black and white ones. First, your child uses a pencil to draw into the styrofoam the image of a minibeast. Then cover the drawing with black paint, turn it over, and press the print onto the paper with the brayer. As with any print-making, continuing to print more copies from just one application of paint makes interesting and varied prints.

SKILLS

✓ Observation

✓ Collecting and recording data

✓ Imaginative thinking

✓ Drawing and painting

Is the Earth Flat?

SKILLS

✓ Asking questions

✓ Observation

✓ Making a hypothesis

✓ Experimenting

✓ Drawing conclusions

The concept of space is too abstract for young children to tackle, despite all the "extraterrestrial" spaceship themes in popular culture. Many books are available with pictures depicting the solar system, but it is still a very difficult idea to grasp the reality that, for example, the earth is round. One way to demonstrate the earth's roundness can be done using the globe. Make some small paper boats with your child and use straws for masts. If the earth is round and the boat begins its journey in Venezuela, it should only be seen coming gradually over the horizon to New York. Place the boat in South America and keep it touching the globe as it moves up toward New York. If you're standing to the side, you'll see the boat appear little by little. But if the earth were flat, you would see something different. Use a table for this experiment. Hold the boat below the top of the table and gradually move it up to the top. It arrives all at once, which is because the table top is flat. Does this happen when you're on the beach and look at the horizon?

Globe Trotting

Look at a globe and talk about what the different colors represent. All the water is blue, including the oceans, lakes, and rivers. The continents are various colors, and so are islands. In a way, continents are just huge islands themselves. Talk in general terms about the names of things. It helps if someone you know has traveled to faraway places. Pointing out where Aunt Polly went last year helps give a sense of place to countries. The fundamental concepts to learn, however, are the roundness of the earth and the idea (abstract, indeed) that it is moving through space.

5 & UP

SKILLS

✓ Asking questions

✓ Observation

237

Your Own Globe

SKILLS

✓ Observation

✓ Asking questions

✓ Eye/hand coordination

✓ Drawing and painting

To make your own globe, blow up a large balloon. Then rip newspaper into long vertical strips and make a watery paste of flour and water in a bowl. Dip a strip of newspaper into the paste, hold it over the bowl, and slide two fingers from your other hand from the top to the bottom of the strip to rid it of extra paste. Then position the strips on the balloon and smooth. Keep the tied end of the balloon uncovered, so later it can be hung from a string. Practice makes perfect, but it only makes your globe more interesting if there are crenellations. When the paper is dry (a day or so), look at the globe and do the continents. The simpler the better, and true accuracy is not the point. If you point to Africa, ask your child to paint it pretty big (older children might replicate the actual shape better). Then have him draw North and South America, Europe, and Russia, and so on. Then, whatever small islands your child might want can be painted in. Make sure to save the water till last. You might want to suggest writing some names with magic marker. Then hang your globe from a string someplace where it can "move" in space.

Shadows

The concept of time, including the seasons, can be approached with your child by observing shadows. The nearer the object is to the sun, the bigger the shadow. When an object blocks light, it creates a shadow. So, the position of the sun in the sky makes a difference in the size and position of shadows. Try this: on a large piece of paper, or with chalk on a sidewalk or driveway, outline your child's shadow in the morning, at noon, and in the afternoon. Record the time on each and measure the shadows. Which is the largest? Have the shadows moved to another spot?

SKILLS

✓ Asking questions

✓ Observation

✓ Making a hypothesis

✓ Drawing conclusions

239

Sun Clocks

5 & UP

SKILLS

✓ Observation

✓ Experimenting

✓ Collecting and recording data

✓ Time

Shadows can help us tell time in other ways as well. Think of sundials. You can make your own sundial outside with a stick and some stones. To begin with, synchronize the hours on the sundial with a clock. Drive a stick into the ground in an open spot. Make sure it's a sunny day—the shortcoming of a sun-clock is that it works only when the sun shines! Then check the clock, and check the shadow of the stick. Where the shadow falls, place a stone and write the hour on it. Make sure the hour stone is in the same position as it is on a clock. Check the shadow every hour. If you can't do it every hour, fill in the gaps another time. The result will be a circle of stones that tell the time. This "clock" will be accurate only for one day because the sun strikes the earth at different angles every day.

Water Clocks

You can experiment with making other kinds of clocks as well. These don't depend on the apparent movement of the sun across the sky, but are ways children can create their own devices to measure time.

To make a water clock, fill a basin with water. Then get a plastic frozen food dish and put a pinpoint hole in the center. Place the plate in the water and see how long it takes to sink. Try to match it up with an ordinary clock and adjust the hole so that the plate takes one hour to completely sink. This is a fun way for your child to time something. Stick the plate in the water and do your homework, then when the plate sinks, go out to play!

5 & UP

SKILLS

✓ Observation

✓ Experimenting

✓ Drawing conclusions

✓ Time

Hour Glass

SKILLS

- ✓ Observation
- ✓ Experimenting
- ✓ Drawing conclusions
- ✓ Time

Make an hour or minute clock. Fill a clear plastic bottle with sand. Have another plastic bottle empty nearby. Get a cork that will fit into the necks of both bottles snugly. Help your child punch out a hole through the middle of the cork. You might use a metal turkey trusser or a long thin nail. When the hole is made, insert the cork into the sand-filled bottle and attach the empty bottle to the other end of the cork. Stand the bottles up with the filled bottle on top and check by your clock how long it takes for the sand to fill the bottom bottle. You might need to adjust the cork hole to meet the amount of time you want your "bottle clock" to measure. To make a much smaller version of the clock, you could use those little plastic drink bottles from airplanes and pare a cork down to size with a knife.

Rain and Soil

R ain permeates the earth's surface and settles underground, in rivers, and in oceans. If the rain is to soak into the surface efficiently, it matters what kind of soil there is. Try this experiment. Find two plastic bottles and punch holes in the bottom of each. Fill one with just sand, and the other first with a layer of clay on the bottom and then sand. Then pour water through each. How do the two bottles differ? Determine what kind of local soil you have. If it has clay or a layer of rocks, this affects where the water goes and how long it takes to get there. If you put a hole just above the level of clay in the one bottle and pour water through, you can see how springs originate. The clay blocks the water and it percolates back to the surface as a spring. Of course, finding a spring in your area, or any area, would demonstrate something about the local soil composition and why the spring occurs.

5 & UP

SKILLS

✓ Asking questions

✓ Observation

✓ Making a hypothesis

✓ Experimenting

✓ Drawing conclusions

243

Sunshine

SKILLS

✓ Asking questions

✓ Observation

✓ Making a hypothesis

✓ Experimenting

✓ Drawing conclusions

The sun is just another star in the sky, but it's brightest to us because it's closest. The sun's energy can help and hurt people and other living things. Discuss with your child why we need the sun. Could we live without it? Think about the times of the year in the northeast when there is a lot of sun, such as summer. What happens to plants during this time? Do the same plants continue to grow in winter when there is much less warmth from the sun? Talk about the deserts of the world where the sun shines intensely every day of the year. How does all this sunlight and heat affect the plants? What do people in the desert do to keep cool? They wear white clothes! To demonstrate how white reflects heat and black absorbs it paint one tin can white and another black. Fill the cans with water and put them in the sunlight. Leave them for a day and then use a thermometer to measure the temperature of the water inside the cans. Which is hottest?

Frozen Mobiles

If you're having a spell of really cold weather, it's possible to make mobiles out of ice. Fill an aluminum pie plate halfway-full of water and freeze in your freezer. When it's frozen, place objects to make an interesting design on top. For example, you might add twigs, or seeds, or buttons, or bits of colored tissue paper or cellophane. When this is arranged, add another inch or so of water and freeze again. When frozen, peel away the pie plate, make a hole in the top, add some string and hang it outside the window.

SKILLS

✓ Small motor skills

✓ Observation

✓ Experimenting

✓ Drawing conclusions

✓ Imaginative thinking

Leaves

SKILLS

✓ Observation

✓ Making comparisons

✓ Sorting and classifying

Children love to collect things. As they grow, their ability to observe, compare, and sort and classify things develops as well. Objects in nature are perfect "found objects" for collections. Children not only hone their skills in observing specific features of things, like the very different shapes of leaves, but also notice and appreciate the outside world.

Collecting leaves can lead in many directions. Not only can leaves themselves be gathered and classified, but the trees they come from might be of interest. The seeds or flowers or fruits from the trees can be matched to the leaves and trees as well. In the Fall, there's nothing like collecting leaves. Encourage your child to use her senses of sight and touch. Can you find ten red leaves? Can you find leaves that are shiny? Or smooth? How about fuzzy? When the collections are brought home, you can sort them together. Don't bother about identifying leaves by name with a young child—the point is to encourage an awareness of the similarities and differences he sees.

Looking at Trees

When collecting leaves, don't forget to look up at the trees. Are any leaves still left on the tree and if so, do they match the leaves on the ground? If they don't, can you find the match of leaf and tree? Talk to your child about how this happened. What about the feel of the leaves? Are some drier than others? If you can pull one off a tree, compare it to a fallen one. How are they different and why? What about trees with holes? How do you think the holes got there? Does it seem that bugs like some trees more than others? Can you find adjacent trees where one has holey leaves and the other doesn't? Can you find the bugs themselves, or have they already left?

SKILLS

✓ Observation

✓ Making comparisons

✓ Making a hypothesis

✓ Drawing conclusions

✓ Sorting and classifying

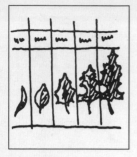

Graphing Leaves

Another leaf activity is to make a graph comparing sizes. On a large sheet of construction paper create five columns. Label the first one "smallest" and the last one "biggest." The in-between ones can each be labeled "bigger." Then spread out all the leaves your child has collected and help her sort and classify her leaves by size. You might want to sort them all before you glue them in their places. Remind your child that probably not all the leaves are going to fit on the graph, so that this might be a good opportunity to choose her favorite ones. It also is a good idea to graph the smallest and the biggest first. The middle ones require subtler judgments to determine size and it's easier to get the obvious ones out of the way first.

Leaf Match

You can make a leaf identification game with your child in any season. Go outside with your child and collect a minimum of five or six different kinds of leaves. Then help your child trace the outlines of these leaves on a large piece of paper. Depending on your interests or your child's age, try to identify each leaf. Then from a collection of leaves, your child can pick out the leaves that match the ones on the paper. Pressing the leaves before doing this exercise help the leaves last longer.

SKILLS

✓ **Making comparisons**

✓ **Observation**

✓ **Sorting and classifying**

Your Own Tree—Early Fall

SKILLS

✓ Observation

✓ Asking questions

✓ Collecting and recording data

✓ Drawing and painting

✓ Sight word recognition

Look around your neighborhood together and find a tree that interests your child. It might be in a park, in front of your apartment house, or in your backyard. A good time to begin this study is in September and it should last one year. Once the tree is selected, start a book about it by drawing a picture. A child of any age can do this. The drawing doesn't have to be representational; your young child can observe things he can't replicate on paper yet. You might also take a photo each month to place beside the drawing. You or your child write the date and maybe a sentence or two about the tree. For example, "There's a nest in it." or "It's the biggest tree," or "The trunk is very smooth." If possible, glue a leaf from it into the book and cover it with contact paper. Maybe you can even find a seed. In such a long study, it's a good idea to know the name of your tree. See if you can help your child identify the tree by looking in a book.

Your Own Tree— Late Fall

For the months of October and November, draw the same tree for each month and write the dates above it. Glue and cover with contact paper another leaf each month. But this time, begin to look for differences in both the leaves and the rest of the tree. In October are there many leaves on the tree? Are there less in November? Write with your child about what she observes. If, in November, there are no leaves at all, see if your child can draw a branch as well as the tree. Examine a branch and look at the buds on it. What will they become in warmer weather?

5 & UP

SKILLS

✓ Observation

✓ Collecting and recording data

✓ Making comparisons

✓ Drawing and painting

✓ Sight word recognition

Your Own Tree— Winter

SKILLS

✓ **Observation**

✓ **Making comparisons**

✓ **Collecting and recording data**

✓ **Drawing and painting**

In December, January, and February, again draw your tree for each month and write the date above it. At each time, look at various areas of the tree and describe what you see. Even if these months have similar weather, it's possible to see changes in your tree. Look at the bark: are there any new holes? How does the bark look with snow on it or if it's wet? Are there any traces of animals anywhere on your tree? Do you ever see an insect, and what about squirrels? Even though it's winter, do you see any birds?

Then zero in on the branches and the buds. Check your December drawing and see if buds look different in February.

Your Own Tree—
Spring and Summer

I n March, when you draw your tree, look carefully at the buds. How are they different from the buds in January? See if you can cut off just one twig and bring it indoors and put it in water. Draw the twig when you first get it and then as it changes. Does the twig in the water indoors bloom faster than the ones on the tree? Why? In April and May, draw and write about all the other changes outside on the tree. Are there blossoms? What happens when they fall off? Does the tree in bloom create much shade? Are there insects crawling in it? How about birds? Does anything grow underneath it? In the summer, maybe there's something you can do to protect the tree, especially if it's in the city. See if you and your neighbor could erect a small fence to keep off dogs, plant flowers, or maybe your child could make a sign identifying the kind of tree it is.

5 & UP

SKILLS

✓ **Asking questions**

✓ **Observation**

✓ **Making comparisons**

✓ **Collecting and recording data**

✓ **Drawing and painting**

253

Neighborhood Trees

SKILLS

✓ Observation

✓ Making comparisons

✓ Collecting and recording data

✓ Drawing and painting

Try doing a neighborhood tree study. Take a walk around your neighborhood with a pencil and paper on a clipboard and draw a simple map of your street and what trees you see with your child. Also, point out and draw a few prominent landmarks, such as buildings and street signs so there is some sort of location involved. The drawings at this point don't have to look anything like trees or buildings, it's where they are that matters. When you get home, get out a big piece of paper, and try to draw the trees very simply in front of the buildings. Then continue to take walks and look for more details, and each time return to your map and fill in what you've found. As you begin to differentiate between the trees, you and your child can draw the particular leaves or types of trunks. As you notice more about them you might want to look them up in a tree book. Then you can write the names of the trees on the map. As your child compares the leaves and shapes of trees and other characteristics, you'll be surprised to find how some names will stick.

Wood Sounds

What about making sounds using only wood? Go on a search for different types and different sizes of wood pieces. Certainly a carpentry shop or a lumberyard can provide a lot of possibilities, but look around the house and outside, as well. Cutting boards, salad bowls, dead tree branches or even twigs might be useful. Suppose some pieces are hollow and others solid, if you tapped each with a spoon or a stick, would the hollow ones create a different sound than the solids? Wet some wood pieces and then hit them with a spoon. Is the sound wet wood makes any different from that made by dry wood? Do you think it's possible to arrange various shapes and kinds of wood in order so that each makes a different sound as you tap it? Try and see.

SKILLS

✓ **Auditory discrimination**

✓ **Experimenting**

✓ **Drawing conclusions**

SKILLS

✓ **Asking questions**

✓ **Observation**

✓ **Collecting and recording data**

✓ **Making comparisons**

✓ **Sorting and classifying**

Wood Museum

To further understand trees, take a close look at wood. Make a small "wood museum" at home with your child. On a table, or in different boxes or trays, arrange items made from wood that you and your child notice from in and out of the house. Are there toothpicks, buttons, toys, picture frames, dishes, utensils, or trivets? Examine the types of wood used in these items and ask your child to describe the characteristics. Do you see the grain of the wood, are there whorls (circular marks), are there knots where branches were once attached? Are some smoother than others? What about colors? After looking and talking about these small objects, try to find the big ones! Help your child make a list of everything in your house that's made of wood (including the house itself). Examine the different appearances of the wood on furniture. Can you feel any grooves? Can you see knots? Does anyone know what kind of tree the dining room table comes from? Or the big bed, or the lamp, or the floor?

Visit a Lumberyard

Take your child to visit a lumberyard, even if you have to take a little trip to get there. Contact them first and ask what time is good for somebody to show you around. There are all kinds of things to learn about wood in such a place and all kinds of questions to ask. Where do they get the wood and how does a tree trunk become those boards? What kinds of trees or wood do they have? What's the difference between evergreen tree wood and oaks or maples? What are all the different machines they use for cutting it at the lumberyard? There's a wealth of sounds and smell there and possibly some free samples to take home.

5 & UP

SKILLS

✓ Asking questions

✓ Observation

Yuck!

SKILLS

✓ Asking questions

✓ Observation

✓ Making a hypothesis

✓ Experimenting

✓ Drawing conclusions

An interesting experiment uses your child's dirty hands! Peel one potato and cut it in half and sterilize two jars and tops. Ask your child to play with the dog or other pet, play in the backyard, or just go about her business for a few hours. Then have her hold one piece of potato for a minute and put it into a jar and label the jar "Dirty Hands." Ask your child to wash her hands, then handle the second piece of potato and put it into the other jar. Label this jar "Clean Hands." Watch the jars for a few days—mold on the "Dirty Hands" should far exceed mold on the clean "Clean Hands" potato.

Catching Some Rays

To help create sparkle in winter windows when sunlight is sparse, make some "sun sparklers." Cut out two circles of clear contact paper. Before removing the backing, have your child cut out various colorful pieces of paper, preferably the see-through kind. Take off the paper backing of one of the circles and have your child stick on his decorations. Then take off the backing from the other circle and press it onto the first one. Make a hole in the top and hang it in a window. Good materials to use are tissue paper and cellophane. Another way to make a sun sparkler is to cut out a circle of cellophane and glue onto it any kind of tissue paper or colored paper you have. This, too, can be hung on a string to a window to catch the sun's rays.

SKILLS

✓ Observation

✓ Drawing conclusions

✓ Imaginative thinking

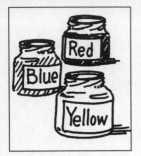

Color Sort

SKILLS

✓ Sorting and classifying

✓ Making comparisons

✓ Experimenting

✓ Drawing conclusions

✓ Language acquisition

Go with your child to a few hardware and paint supply stores and see if you can get a paint sample book or two. An alternative is to ask for chips of different colored paints. When you get home, cut apart all the color squares, mix them up and put them on a tray. If you were lucky enough to get two sample books, a good activity is simply matching the colors by spreading the squares out and sorting them into pairs.

Differentiating between shades of the same color is a subtle task. A good beginning might be to do some paint mixing. Start with red and just add a few drops of white. Gradually increase the white until you reach a light pink. Then see if your child can find shades of red and other colors among the paint chips.

Nature Color Match

Ask in your local hardware store for some panels of paint chips. These can be used in all sorts of activities. One is seasonal, to be used outdoors. For this, take a few panels with you and go for a nature walk. See how many natural items you and your child can find that match the chips. Be sure to have some earth hues with you in any season, particularly in the fall. But bring along brighter shades as well. It's more of a challenge in the colder months to discover red or yellow outdoors, but it's possible if you hunt. Of course, in Fall, take the reds, yellows, and oranges. See what particular shades match particular leaves. In summer, the subtlest job would be to match the shades of green that are so abundant. The chips themselves could be cut and glued to a chart and the color source could be written next to it. But just walking around and matching is an engrossing activity, especially when you're looking for a very specific shade of a color.

5 & UP

SKILLS

✓ Observation

✓ Visual discrimination

✓ Making comparisons

✓ Sorting and classifying

261

Animal Hunt

Go on a neighborhood animal hunt. In the city, beside dogs and cats, you might notice squirrels, mice, or rats, an occasional boa constrictor on someone's shoulders, and of course, birds. The suburbs offer skunks, raccoons, and snakes. The country offers everything if you know how to look. Photos can be taken of neighborhood animals, and drawings can be made. A map of the general neighborhood environment could be drawn on a large sheet of paper and these photos or drawings can be glued to the area where the animals were seen. If you have binoculars, let your child spy with them. A simpler focusing tool can be a toilet paper tube. This helps define a spot for children and leaves out the extraneous surroundings. On the map or mounted photo or drawing, your child can describe the features of the animal, if it was eating and what, and how it reacted to people being so near. Doing some research in books at home or in the library, assisted by a grownup, could add even more to what is already known.

Visiting Animals

Visit a pet shop as well as the zoo. Try to go at feeding times to the zoo, so that the zoo personnel can provide extra information about the animals they're caring for. But a pet shop offers more opportunity to interview the people who work there. There is often a wide array of animals in stores, and children can categorize them into groups. How many types of fish, how many reptiles, rodents, or amphibians? Then, by observation, and by asking the attendants, children could make lists of the animals, their food, their characteristics, how old they are and where they come from. It might also be interesting to find out how many people work in the store and how often they feed and care for all the animals there.

5 & UP

SKILLS

✓ Asking questions

✓ Observation

✓ Collecting and recording data

✓ Making comparisons

263

SKILLS

- ✓ Asking questions
- ✓ Observation
- ✓ Making comparisons
- ✓ Collecting and recording data
- ✓ Drawing and painting

Animal Studies

At any age it is interesting for a child to learn about animals. For a very young child, just discovering (with your help and from a book) that squirrels often build leafy nests at the tops of trees is an important fact, especially since birds build nests as well. For the older child, it might be interesting to observe the nests more carefully and to describe the differences. This could lead to discoveries about birds' nests in general and how they differ from each other. Children are curious, and asking questions and finding answers can be very satisfying. While identifying animals (including birds) in the neighborhood or visiting a zoo or pet shop, your child is bound to pick up information about various animals. Do some simple research projects about animals that interest your child in particular. You can go to the library or bookstore and look up a particular animal or two and make a scrapbook with the information. You can also use magazine pictures, a photo, or a drawing to illustrate the page. Keep it simple and appropriate to your child's interests. A one- or two-fact description of the animal would certainly add to your child's knowledge of the animal kingdom.

Animal Match

Another way to use animal information in a game is to make "Animal Match." Choose with your child ten or more animals that she knows something about. Then make four or more large bingo cards by drawing or gluing pictures or photos of these different animals on each card. Make sure each card has a different arrangement of animals as well as a few animals that are different from those on the other cards. Each card should have six or nine pictures on it. Then make up a list of animal clues or descriptions for each animal represented. When the game is ready, have one child (or adult) be the caller and read the clues. If the child has that particular animal on her card, she can put a button on its picture. The first person to fill up the card wins.

5 & UP

SKILLS

✓ Collecting and recording data

✓ Critical thinking

✓ Language acquisition

Animal Magnets

SKILLS

✓ Observation

✓ Imaginative thinking

✓ Eye/hand coordination

✓ Drawing and painting

Favorite animals (or anything else for that matter) can be made out of special play clay and fashioned into refrigerator magnets. The dough needs to be cooked first. For about twenty animals mix 4 cups of baking soda, 2 cups of cornstarch, and 2.5 cups water together in a pot and cook over medium heat, stirring constantly for about 10 minutes. After about 10 minutes, turn it out on a dish and cover with a damp dishtowel. When it's cool, knead it into a ball. This dough can be stored in the refrigerator in a plastic bag.

On a piece of waxed paper, flatten a lump of dough with your hand until it's about 1/4 inch thick. You can use animal cookie cutters or design your own, but be careful not to add long skinny tails that might break when dry. You can add small pieces of dough for features by gently pressing them in. Then let the animal dry overnight. Next day paint it with either poster paint or acrylic paint and when this is dry, glue a small magnet (or two) on the back.

Drink Your Milk!

All animals known as mammals produce milk to feed their babies. Human beings, of course, are mammals, and some children may have had the experience of seeing a sibling or other baby being breast-fed or, of course, remember themselves being breast-fed. It's an interesting topic to discover other mammals feeding their babies and also interesting to focus on the other milk we humans drink for most of our lives. Talk about this with your child. Most children will know it's cow's milk, but most will probably not know that some people drink sheep's milk and that camel milk is popular with people in the desert. Of course, goat's milk has a following in this country as well, and it would be an interesting experiment to sample some and compare it to cow's milk. A good discussion to have is about foods made from milk. Don't forget to include cheese from goat's milk as well (and sample it.).

SKILLS

✓ Asking questions

✓ Observation

✓ Critical thinking

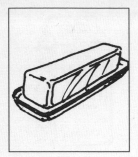

Making Butter

Both making butter and making cheese are wonderful lessons in change. From a familiar product like milk, completely different products emerge. This certainly helps young children know what foods you can make from milk and have the experience of doing it themselves.

Instead of using whole milk, just the fatty part or cream is used in making butter. Buy whipping cream and fill some baby food jars about two-thirds full with the cream. Then fasten the lids well and shake, shake, shake! It might take up to ten or fifteen minutes, so be prepared to have some backups for shaking. The watery liquid called whey will separate from the butter when the butter is ready. Pour it off and enjoy!

Cottage Cheese

You can make cottage cheese as well. Place milk in a warm place for a day or two until it turns sour. Pull up a chair and place the seat on a table. Tie a piece of cheese cloth on each of the four legs of the chair and pour or set the sour milk in the center of the cheese cloth to drip into a bowl underneath. By the end of the day the whey will have drained into the bowl and the cheese cloth (appropriately called) will be full of cottage cheese.

4 & UP

SKILLS

✓ Observation

✓ Making a hypothesis

✓ Experimenting

✓ Drawing conclusions

Plant Life

✓ Asking questions

✓ Observation

✓ Making a hypothesis

✓ Experimenting

✓ Collecting and recording data

✓ Drawing conclusions

To show your child what living things need to grow, you can do a simple experiment with three plants. Discuss with your child before you start what he thinks a plant needs to survive. Sunshine? Water? Soil? Make a list of all the different ideas that he has. Choose one, for example, sunshine, and say "Let's do an experiment and see what we can find out!" Plant some fast-growing seeds such as radishes in three different pots and place them near a window where they can get some sun. As the first leaves appear, move one of the pots to a shady corner of the room and place another pot in the closet. Continue to water all the plants regularly (every other day) and talk about your observations. Keep a log book and record what you see. Your child can draw pictures of the plants for the log book or you can take photographs and glue them in the book. When you've determined that, yes, plants do need sunshine to live, you might want to save the plants that are dying and put them back next to the window. If you time this right, you can watch your two dying plants come back to life.

Vegetable Garden

Here's an idea for an indoor root vegetable garden that you can do with your child. First, cut off the top inch of a parsnip, turnip, beet, sweet potato, or carrot. Make sure to keep a bit of the green stems on the top, as well. These tops of root vegetables can then be planted in a shallow dish with a layer of pebbles. Fill the dish with about a ¼ inch of water and watch for leaves!

4 & UP

SKILLS

✓ Observation

✓ Making a hypothesis

✓ Experimenting

✓ Drawing conclusions

Carrot Top

SKILLS

✓ Observation

✓ Making a hypothesis

✓ Experimenting

✓ Drawing conclusions

One way to grow a carrot is to cut off the top end to about 2 inches, turn it upside down and with a vegetable peeler scoop out the center. Make sure your hole will hold 2 teaspoons of water. Then poke 3 toothpicks into the outside of the vegetable and tie a string to each one, fill the hole with water and hang your carrot from a hook in a window. All the shoots and leaves will emerge from the stem part and form a hanging plant. Keep the hole filled with water.

Grow a Grapefruit!

Grapefruit seeds make beautiful plants with very aromatic leaves. The best seeds to plant seem to be in grapefruit you eat in the summer, and the seeds are often greenish and sometimes even have a beginning of a root. But you can try winter fruit as well. Plant these in any pot, but the bigger the better because the plant will eventually be large. Sometimes though, it's a problem to remember to water what appears to be an empty pot, so trick yourself by sticking a seed or two in a pot with a plant in it that you water regularly. Then, when you notice the grapefruit seeds sprouting, carefully scoop them out and plant them in their own pots.

SKILLS

✓ Observation

✓ Making a hypothesis

✓ Experimenting

✓ Drawing conclusions

SKILLS

✓ **Observation**

✓ **Making a hypothesis**

✓ **Experimenting**

✓ **Drawing conclusions**

Cold Storage

Certain fruit seeds can be planted indoors only if you "winterize" them first. If you put them in the refrigerator, the cold will mimic the winter they would normally experience outdoors, so get some apple seeds, or peach pits, or plum pits and put them in a container in the refrigerator for two months. Then plant them in pots, put them in a sunny window, and watch for sprouts. One bit of good advice is to buy only organic fruit that has not been treated with chemicals that might interfere with development.

Sprouts

Any seed that begins to grow is sprouting. But the "sprouts" you can buy at the grocery store are edible and usually grown from beans. These are particularly rich in nutrients and fun to grow on your own. To sprout bean seeds, use lentils, pigeon peas, or mung beans. These are good fool-proof sprouters. Use a different jar for each kind of bean. In a glass jar put a handful of beans and cover with water. Cover the top of the jar with a small piece of cheesecloth fixed with a rubber band. After 8 hours (overnight is good) pour the water out, hold the jar under the faucet and rinse with fresh water. Shake this out and let beans stand overnight again and repeat this rinsing process. Remember the only time the seeds sit in water is the first night. Every morning and every evening, rinse the seeds until you see them sprout, which will take a week or so. Stick them in a salad, or in pita bread or just eat them by the handful. Recently, some commercial sprouts have been found to be contaminated with bacteria, so all the more reason to make your own.

SKILLS

✓ Asking questions

✓ Observation

✓ Making a hypothesis

✓ Experimenting

✓ Drawing conclusions

Sound Survey

SKILLS

✓ Observation

✓ Auditory
  discrimination

✓ Imaginative
  thinking

Do a sound survey. Sit quietly indoors and listen for sounds. Point out the sound of a clock ticking. Children are more apt to hear a car's horn, a dog barking, or a sibling singing in another room. But subtler sounds are harder to hear, such as the clock or breathing. Outdoors, there will probably be cars, people talking, footsteps. But what about the wind, the birds, the rustle of trees and plants? When your child hears a sound, see if she can describe it. Is it a chirp of a bird, a screech of a car, a whoosh of the wind? Which sounds are loud, and which are soft? Are there any that are scary or some that are pleasant?

Making Sounds

Inside the house, find things to make sounds with. Aside from banging a pencil, shaking the peppercorns in the grinder, what about inventing sources of sound? How about filling a box with pebbles or pennies? Or filling bottles of different shapes with various amounts of water and tapping them? Or crumpling different kinds of paper, such as newspaper, tissue paper? Can you help your child describe these sounds? Which are loud, which are soft? A good game is to tap a series of six or seven things (a window, the refrigerator, the floor, etc.) and then close your eyes while your child taps them in a different order. Can you guess where the sound comes from?

4 & UP

SKILLS

✓ **Experimenting**

✓ **Drawing conclusions**

✓ **Auditory discrimination**

277

Changing Sounds

SKILLS

✓ **Experimenting**

✓ **Drawing conclusions**

✓ **Auditory discrimination**

Another sound activity is to experiment with how far a sound can travel. Tap a spoon against a glass and keep walking away from your child while you do it. See how far you have to go before she can't hear the tapping. Suppose you asked your child to lie on the floor with her ear pressed to it while you tap on the floor. What does the sound sound like to her? Then try it without lying on the floor. How is the sound different? Can sound go through things, then? To extend this activity, how about tapping a water pipe, while she holds her ear to it, and then again when she's sitting across the room. How is the sound different? Does the sound go through the pipe?

Water Everywhere

Turn on the faucet and ask your child where he thinks the water is coming from. Depending on where you live there are all sorts of explorations to be done if you want to trace your water source. First of all, do you have your own water supply from a well? If so, your questions will be about how wells are made, how deep they are, and where the water under the earth comes from. Asking neighbors to determine how deep and efficient their wells are is a useful tool. Why do wells relatively near each other provide different amounts of water? The question of where waste water goes after it's used is also important. In the country does someone other than the well person need to be contacted about this? All these explanations to do with country water supplies will differ according to the age of your child and how much you yourself want to tackle. From a discussion of where rain goes to how it filters into different kinds of soil, to looking at maps and identifying bodies of water or comparing fresh and salt water sources, you and your child can open up an entire area of information that normally is overlooked, especially for young children.

5 & UP

SKILLS

✓ Asking questions

✓ Observation

279

Drops of Water 1

SKILLS

✓ Asking questions

✓ Observation

✓ Making a hypothesis

✓ Experimenting

✓ Drawing conclusions

Experimenting with drops of water is an interesting activity. Begin by dipping a straw into water and putting your finger over the open hole at the top. If you lift the straw from the water holding your finger in place, water will remain in the straw. Lift your finger and let a drop of water fall on a surface. What shape is the water? Suppose you make a row of drops and examine their sizes. Are they the same? How can you manage the straw to change the size of the water drops? How do you make the largest? And the smallest?

Drops of Water 2

Make water drops with other materials. If you used a pin, would the drops be smaller? What about toothpicks, forks, pencils? Experiment with size as well as how you can change the drops. Suppose you put two drops so close that they touch each other. If you put a drop of water on the print of a newspaper, does it magnify the letters? If you dropped the water or a piece of waxed paper or a piece of glass, you could experiment with the size of the drop and magnification. This "lens" needs to be lifted at different heights to get the clearest view of letters or words. Do bigger drops create more magnification?

SKILLS

✓ Asking questions

✓ Observation

✓ Making a hypothesis

✓ Experimenting

✓ Drawing conclusions

Water and Pipes

If you live in a developed area, water sources are hard to identify and easy to ignore. Looking at maps, especially local ones, provides a beginning. If you can find the reservoir that supplies your water, it would be worth the trip. Contacting the local water company also will help answer such questions as how water is purified and how it's carried right to your doors. This involves the discovery of pumps. The whole system of pipes that tie the water supply together is an interesting area for children to explore. Do it on a very local level—your own building. After establishing the basic water source (usually a reservoir), examine the pipes in the building. You could trace them from the boiler, a water heater in the basement, up through the house or apartment. Where are the water pipes for the tub, the kitchen sink, the washing machine? Of course, most pipes are covered, but not entirely, if you really look. Your child might be interested in drawing (with your help) the system of water pipes where you live.

Bubbles!

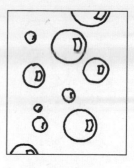

Make some bubbles! To begin with, mix about 8 tablespoons of dishwashing liquid to a quart of water in a jar. You can make your own loop (like the ones from commercial bubble mix) from a strip of wire. Twist it into a circle at one end and you have your loop. But other items can also be used to make bubbles. Try straws, paper tubes, tin cans with each end removed. Dip the object into the soap solution, check to see that the dipped end has a film of soap across it, and blow, gently at first. Then make some observations. Are all the bubble shapes the same? What happens if you touch the bubble with your finger? Suppose you dipped your finger into the soap mixture first? In which direction do bubbles float? Look at the surface of the bubbles. What colors do you see? What if you added food color to the soap solution? What color bubbles do you get?

5 & UP

SKILLS

✓ **Asking questions**

✓ **Observation**

✓ **Experimenting**

✓ **Drawing conclusions**

283

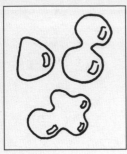

Bubble Shapes

5 & UP

SKILLS

✓ Asking questions

✓ Observation

✓ Making a hypothesis

✓ Experimenting

✓ Drawing conclusions

Get some pliable wire from a hardware store and bend pieces of it into all kinds of different shapes. You could make a figure 8, a triangle, or a spiral. Try some free-form ones, too. Then dip each one into a shallow dish of soap bubble solution and blow on the soap film. What kinds of shapes are the bubbles?

What about looking at your reflection in the soap bubble film before you blow on it? What's the difference between looking in the mirror and looking in soap film? Suppose your friend puts his face behind the soap film, and then moves further away from it. How does this change the way his face looks?

Eye Droppers and Water

U se eye droppers to drop water into different surfaces. You could include the kitchen counter, the chopping board, your hand, or the floor. Also, you could arrange an assortment of materials on a table. One thing to observe is what the drops look like when they land on different things. The other observation could be what materials absorb water and what materials resist it. The various materials could include aluminum foil, a sponge, a piece of plastic, a washcloth, newspaper, or construction paper. Encourage your child to describe what happens to the drops. Some drops will be absorbed quickly, some will take some time, others will just stay on the surface.

5 & UP

SKILLS

✓ Observation

✓ Experimenting

✓ Drawing conclusions

Hearing Test

SKILLS

✓ **Asking questions**

✓ **Experimenting**

✓ **Drawing conclusions**

✓ **Auditory discrimination**

Here's an activity that tests your hearing. Have your child blindfold herself or a friend. The blindfolded child needs to guess what the other child is dropping. Gather a number of objects that sound differently on impact—in itself a fruitful exercise for your child. Try an eraser, a ball, a pillow. Or what about a dime and a quarter? Is it possible to differentiate the sounds and tell which coin it is? Maybe not. But if you practiced first without the blindfold using only coins you might build up your expertise so that when blindfolded you might be able to distinguish one from the other.

Taping Sounds

Use the tape recorder to record ordinary sounds around the house and see how many your child can recognize. Try running water into the bathtub, sweeping a floor, or petting your cat as she purrs. Or snap your fingers, lock the door, close the refrigerator, or shuffle your feet. Is it possible to guess the replayed sounds? After your child has a try, maybe she'll enjoy recording different sounds and having you guess. Would it make any difference if the volume is low or high? Experiment together and test the listening skills of your family.

5 & UP

SKILLS

✓ **Experimenting**

✓ **Drawing conclusions**

✓ **Auditory discrimination**

287

Soda Bottle Terrarium

SKILLS

✓ Observation

✓ Imaginative thinking

✓ Eye/hand coordination

Suppose you wanted to replicate a piece of the woods in your own house. Besides collecting soil, stones, plants, and maybe even animals from outside, you'd have to have a terrarium to put it all in. Instead of doing the easy thing and buying one, making your own terrarium can be fun. All kinds of glass or plastic containers will suffice—from fishbowls to gallon jars to plastic soda bottles. A two-liter soda bottle is particularly suited for a small terrarium, and it's certainly the right price. After rinsing one thoroughly, cut off the top about two inches down with a knife or scissors. Then pull off the hard plastic bottom—if this is too hard, soak it for a bit in warm water. Then use this bottom part for the bottom of the terrarium. When you've arranged your soil and plants in it, simply place the clear plastic bottle part upside down over the plants and put the whole thing in a window where it will get some sun in the morning or afternoon. Too much sun doesn't work for woodland plants.

Terrariums

When planting a terrarium in a
container larger than a soda bottle,
cover the bottom of the terrarium with
gravel, or sand, or a layer of small pebbles.
Then you have a choice of using soil from
the woods or buying potting soil at the
store. In any case, add about two or 3
inches of soil. Then go into the woods and
look for small plants that will have a natural
look when planted in your container.
Observe the various kinds of small plants
on the ground and notice the contours of
the ground. For a miniature forest, you
might want to have a slight hill or two and
certainly some stones and twigs.

SKILLS

✓ **Observation**

✓ **Imaginative
thinking**

✓ **Eye/hand
coordination**

✓ Observation

✓ Imaginative
thinking

✓ Eye/hand
coordination

Miniature Forest

Another possibility for your terrarium is to add a small container of water and submerge it to create a "pond." When you select plants, be careful to bring the soil around the roots with the plants and press them down carefully in the terrarium. Make sure they stay moist and out of strong sunlight. Tiny tree seedlings are also a good choice. Perhaps you'll see a tiny maple tree, or certainly an evergreen like a pine tree or a cedar in the woods. Lichens, which grow on rocks or tree trunks, are another good choice, as well as mosses spread over the floor of the woods. Be sure to take a piece of whatever the plant is growing on when you take lichens or mosses. Over the top of the terrarium you need a glass cover, so the plants remain moist. But don't seal it entirely, because mold might develop. Stick a piece of cardboard under each corner of the glass cover so air can circulate. You will need to spray some water in once every week or two.

Woodland Creatures

If you'd like a woodland creature in your terrarium, frogs, toads, or salamanders are a good choice. If you're patient, you can spot these creatures in the woods and bring one home. All of these amphibians can be caught with a small net and then placed in a covered box for the journey home. Make sure your terrarium resembles the habitat the animal comes from. A good-size aquarium is the best container, and a dish of water is always necessary. In the woods, frogs and toads eat insects, slugs, worms, or snails. Those in terrariums will also eat raw meat and fish. They should be fed every day or two in summer and less often in winter. In a year or so, these animals might be too large to be captive, so take them to a pond and set them free. All of these terrariums (actually called vivariums, because they have animals inside), need to be covered tightly with fine screening. You can either attach the screen to a good frame, or bend the screening over the edges after the corners are cut out.

SKILLS

✓ Observation

✓ Eye/hand coordination

291

Puddle Wonderful

SKILLS

✓ Asking questions

✓ Observation

✓ Experimenting

✓ Drawing conclusions

Puddles are always exciting for children! Go out with your child and find some after a rain. Observe the things that are reflected in it, maybe the sky, or surrounding trees, or your faces. Notice the pattern the water makes when a pebble is thrown in. Circular patterns are everywhere in nature, perhaps you might begin to notice them elsewhere. Experiment with floating objects in the water. What about leaves, twigs, or stones? If the weather is going to remain clear, ask your child to draw a circle around the puddle with chalk. Then come back at the end of the day and notice what has happened. Keep the explanations and the vocabulary simple. The definition of evaporation is that the water disappears into the air. You can use the example of drying clothes on a clothesline. What happens to the water there?

292

Two of a Kind

Here's a hands-on activity that helps both develop visual discrimination skills and reinforce some information that your child has learned about natural objects she's found. From her collection of natural materials, such as seeds or leaves, pick six or more and put them on a tray. Then, without her seeing you, put matches of these items around the room. Ask your child to look at the items in the tray for one minute or less, and then hide the tray and ask him to find the matches. When he finds something, encourage him to use the names and to provide descriptions, such as "I found the maple seed" or "this is the white rock with a hole in it."

5 & UP

SKILLS

✓ **Observation**

✓ **Visual discrimination**

✓ **Language acquisition**

293

Finding a Match

Another way to enhance visual memory is to find duplicates of natural objects outside. From a collection of leaves, seeds, and flowers that you have in the house, select one or two specimens; for example, an oak leaf or a chestnut, and take them with you to find their matches on a walk outside with your child. This will give you an opportunity to mention the name of the leaf or seed, notice which tree produces which seed, as well as help your child develop visual discrimination.

Focusing in On . . .

Binoculars can be difficult to use for young children; but so can focusing on one particular object without some kind of support. If you're looking for nests, spotting birds, or would like your child to really notice the characteristics of one specific leaf, take along a paper towel tube. Looking through one of these limits distractions and allows the child to look at one thing at a time. To demonstrate, you could start with the child's thumb. Ask her to look just at it through the tube and describe it. Can she see the whorls on the back and the lines underneath the nail? What about the cut on its side? Then switch to a flower or a stone or a nest. After talking about her observations, your child might want to draw what she remembers.

5 & UP

SKILLS

✓ Visual discrimination

✓ Observation

✓ Drawing and painting

Outside Sounds

SKILLS

✓ Asking questions

✓ Experimenting

✓ Auditory discrimination

✓ Critical thinking

Have you ever considered taping the sounds outside your house? Regardless of where you live you can find quiet and noisy places nearby, or you can simply tape sounds at the same place but at different times of the day. Traffic sounds, construction noise, people walking and talking are all part of a typical soundtrack in the city, but if you taped them at a busy time of day and then on a weekend, it can be interesting to compare the differences. In the country, the same thing can be done, but some of the sounds might be more subtle. Consider placing the microphone in some tall grass or under the tree where the bird feeder is. All kinds of delightful guessing games might evolve from these recordings. Imagine a "seasonal" sound tape with crickets, the snow plow, the barbecue, or basketballs bouncing. What about sounds at night near your house compared to sounds in the middle of the day? Listening to these tapes will certainly sharpen your child's awareness of all the sounds that are usually just taken for granted.

Country Sounds

I f you live in the country or even in the suburbs, it might be interesting for your child to hear how many small sounds there are outside that are just taken for granted. Suppose you taped the morning or evening songs of birds, particularly in the summer? If you've got water nearby, is it possible to hear what sounds it makes? What about the wind, the sound of trees, branches moving in it? You might help your child make comparisons of sounds at morning or night or even during different kinds of weather.

5 & UP

SKILLS

✓ Observation

✓ Auditory discrimination

✓ Critical thinking

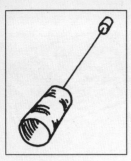

SKILLS

✓ **Experimenting**

✓ **Drawing conclusions**

✓ **Auditory discrimination**

Phone Me

Did you ever make a "telephone" when you were a child so that you and a friend might converse secretly? Well, the idea is still a good one for your own child. Metal is the best conductor of the vibrations that voices make, so get two tin cans and make a hole in the bottom of each with a nail. Be careful of sharp edges, either around the hole, or around the open end of the can. Putting some electrical tape around the edges will eliminate the possibility of cuts. Then thread a piece of string through the two holes and decide how long you want this phone cord to go. Knot the string at each end and proceed to have a conversation.

Two-Way Conversation

Another way to make a phone is to use two metal funnels and some plastic tubing that will fit inside the opening of the funnels. It's a good idea to buy enough of this at the hardware store so that the two children using the phone can be at least 10 feet away from each other for a conversation. Metal amplifies sound and the idea of standing out of sight from your friend and talking on a homemade phone while the other holds her phone to her ear is lots of fun!

SKILLS

✓ **Experimenting**

✓ **Drawing conclusions**

✓ **Auditory discrimination**

✓ **Small motor skills**

Rock Collections

SKILLS

✓ Observation

✓ Collecting and recording data

✓ Sorting and classifying

✓ Making comparisons

There are lots of interesting activities to do with rocks and stones. Rocks are fascinating to collect and it's very natural for a child to make comparisons about his collection, but you can help organize ways of looking at rocks with your child. One observation you can make is to notice the very different colors rocks have when they are wet. You could also sort them by color, size, or shape. Touch the rocks and describe their attributes. Do they feel cool or smooth? What about cracks, holes, or sharp edges in your rocks? Maybe you can make a group of only round, white ones.

Flower Dyes

To make beautiful natural dyes to use in painting or on cloth, go outside and gather two dozen or so marigolds. Cut off the stems and put the flowers in a big pot covered with water and simmer for two or more hours. Remove the flowers and add one cup of apple cider vinegar to set the dye. When it cools, use the dye for painting delicate drawings for bookmarks or small drawings. Use very fine brushes. You can also dip pieces of cloth into the dye to make doilies or hangings. To decorate them you can use oil or water based inks when they're dry.

SKILLS

✓ Observation

✓ Imaginative thinking

✓ Drawing and painting

✓ Eye/hand coordination

SKILLS

✓ **Observation**

✓ **Collecting and recording data**

✓ **Language acquisition**

✓ **Estimating**

✓ **Drawing and painting**

Buds in Bloom

In early spring, take a walk with your child and look at buds. Explain that they've been there all winter, but the warm weather will make them grow. Find a few buds that you want to watch. Perhaps you know that some are on an apple tree, a maple tree, a forsythia bush, but it doesn't matter if you don't know the name of the plant. Have your child tie some yarn near the bud or buds so it will be obvious which ones you're observing. Talk about what you think will happen. Estimate how long it will take before it will completely bloom. Your child could keep a record of the buds and draw how they look at different intervals. Be sure to write down the date in your record book, as well as any observations you make.

Mystery Rainbow

I t's hard to believe, but the color black contains all the colors of a rainbow! To prove this, get a coffee filter and fold it over 3 or 4 times. Draw a thick line about an inch from the end of this shape with a black water-based pen. Put this end of the filter into a cup with a small amount of water and watch as the colors that are hidden in the black line move up into the filter after a few hours or even sooner.

SKILLS

✓ **Asking questions**

✓ **Observation**

✓ **Making a hypothesis**

✓ **Experimenting**

✓ **Drawing conclusions**

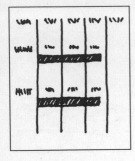

Weather Graph

SKILLS

✓ Observation

✓ Eye/hand coordination

✓ Drawing and painting

✓ Graphing

A roll of adding machine paper can be used for all kinds of activities. To begin with, cut a strip 3 or 4 feet long. Divide up the strip into fourteen or more equal sections using a marker. This can be taped on a wall and made into a weather graph. Each day talk about the weather with your child. You might also read the forecast in the newspaper to him or watch the one on TV. Ask your child to make up symbols for various kinds of weather, such as a sun for sunny days, or a bending tree for windy days. Then each day, ask him to record what he observes in a section, and when a week full of weather has accumulated, talk about the results. Were most days sunny, or was there a lot of rain? Keep this graph going for a while to observe weather patterns. You could write the month along the top or even write the dates underneath each picture.

Outdoor Painting

To develop motor skills and understand the concept of evaporation, give your child a bucket of water and paint brush and have her go outside to "paint" on a nice day. Perhaps she could paint the terrace, or the wall of the house, or a fence, or the sidewalk. Talk about how the "paint" or water disappears into the air. Use the word "evaporate," but you don't belabor it. This is an especially interesting activity to do on a sunny day, when evaporation will happen quickly. Repeat the activity on a rainy, humid day. Ask your child what the difference in evaporation is in such different weather. Why does she think the water disappeared more quickly when the sun was shining?

SKILLS

✓ Observation

✓ Critical thinking

✓ Small motor skills

305

Make Your Own Dirt!

SKILLS

✓ **Asking questions**

✓ **Observation**

✓ **Making a hypothesis**

✓ **Experimenting**

✓ **Drawing conclusions**

You can make your own soil if you can find some sedimentary rocks like sandstone in your area. Sedimentary rocks are formed of layers of sediments or grains and are common in much of North America. Put a small piece of sandstone in a plastic container along with a harder rock like granite and ask your child to take turns with someone else shaking the two together. You will gradually see the sandstone break down and become grains again. Of course, all rocks exposed to the elements eventually break down into soil, but sedimentary rocks are the most vulnerable. Incidentally, the brownstone houses of New York City and other cities are actually made of sandstone.

Ecosystems

A tree has many characteristics of its own, but it also creates an entire environment for other living things. Find a particular tree and look carefully at all the life surrounding it. Are there any squirrel or birds' nests? Is there any sign of woodpecker holes in the bark? Check carefully to find insects or spiders on the trunk or leaves or on the ground beneath it. Are there any fallen leaves on the ground? Dig around the ground and see if you can uncover any earthworms. Worms eat dead leaves, so they are often residents of a tree's environment. All these living things depend on each other and form an entire ecosystem.

5 & UP

SKILLS

✓ Asking questions

✓ Observations

✓ Drawing conclusions

Magnet Survey

SKILLS

✓ **Observation**

✓ **Experimenting**

✓ **Drawing conclusions**

✓ **Critical thinking**

Have a discussion with your child about how magnets are used. Obviously, they hold things up on the refrigerator, and magnetic letters and numbers are familiar. Maybe he has some toys that contain magnets, such as cars or trains. But what about pot holders or a magnetic paperclip holder? If you use an electric can opener, observe what happens to the lid after it's removed. You could make a list with your child of all the ways magnets are useful. Suppose you dropped a lot of pins in the grass, what would be the easiest way to pick them up?

Magnet Info

Store-bought magnets are made of steel. The two points on every magnet where power is the greatest are called the north and south poles. If you try to bring the north pole of one magnet into contact with the north pole of another magnet, they will repel each other. But if the north pole of a magnet is brought close to the south pole of another, they will attract each other. It's important to remember that if a magnet gets dropped it can lose its magnetism and that magnets should be kept away from computer and TV screens.

SKILLS

✓ Observation

✓ Experimenting

✓ Drawing conclusions

309

Magnet Attractions

SKILLS

✓ Asking questions

✓ Observation

✓ Experimenting

✓ Drawing conclusions

✓ Sorting and classifying

A simple experiment with magnets is to find objects that a magnet will attract. Gather a range of different objects such as nails, keys, paperclips, staples, aluminum foil, and metal scissors. Ask your child to sort the objects into two groups, those that magnets attract and those that don't. Children might think that anything metal will be picked up by a magnet, so this experiment will be of interest to them. Explain that magnets attract only metal things made of iron, so the sorted piles are really piles of iron things and of metals not made with iron. (Magnets will also pick up cobalt and nickel, but these are not common.)

Magnet Poles

To demonstrate that magnets are strongest at the poles, put a lot of paperclips in a box. Then ask your child to place a bar magnet in the box with the paperclips. What happens when the magnet is removed? Talk about what you see and explain what it proves. If your child removes all the paperclips and then runs just one along the bar magnet, she will discover the strongest pull at each pole. Try to obtain some differently shaped magnets to experiment with. Regardless of the shape, you will discover that the strongest pull is always at the ends.

SKILLS

✓ Asking questions

✓ Observation

✓ Experimenting

✓ Drawing conclusions

SKILLS

✓ Asking questions

✓ Observation

✓ Experimenting

✓ Drawing conclusions

Magnetic Power

Make a small boat out of a cork and add a toothpick for the mast and a paper sail. Then attach either a paperclip or a nail or a thumbtack to it, and place it in a small container of water. Ask your child to move a magnet near the container and he'll discover that he can make the boat move. This proves that a magnet's force can go through materials.

Why not try other materials? How about a piece of wood, cardboard, dirt, or sand? Suppose you cover a nail in a bowl of sand and try to fish it out with a magnet. Would it come to the surface? Vary the amount of sand or dirt on the bowl. Put a paperclip in a glass of water. Will a magnet be able to get it out without touching it?

Make a Magnet

Can you make a nail into a magnet?
Get a large nail and a flat magnet.
Touch the top of the nail to the magnet
and stroke the nail across the magnet
from one end to the other for a minute or
so. Then see if the nail will pick up some
paperclips. You could try various nails and
see if this will work on all of them.
Another observation to make is how long
the nail will remain magnetized. Set the
timer or look at the clocks and arrive at
some times to check on the nail. How
long does the nail stay a magnet?

5 & UP

SKILLS

✓ **Asking questions**

✓ **Observation**

✓ **Making a hypothesis**

✓ **Experimenting**

✓ **Drawing conclusions**

Zooming In on Birds

Studying birds is fascinating to children. Most people don't realize it, but the definition of a bird is "if it has feathers, it's a bird." Children think of flying as a requisite, but what about penguins or ostriches? Learning about birds can be a two-pronged effort: discovering general characteristics of all birds, and then zooming in on a few specific ones. Usually the choice of which birds to study comes from your own environment and the birds that live there, but exotic ones from zoos and pet stores might also be a choice.

What Makes a Bird a Bird

Looking at the bodies of birds is a logical beginning for the study of birds. You might get some bird books for children out of the library for more information. Certainly, birds' eyes are curious organs. Their vision is better than ours and each eye can see separate things. Noticing beaks is a crucial part of identifying birds, and their shape reveals the type of food the bird eats. But if you think of birds that fly, it's fun to figure out how birds can do it at all. Although wings and feathers obviously matter, what also makes flying happen are bones. Most of a bird's bones are hollow, and therefore light. If you go to the beach, it's often possible to find some bird skeletons, especially heads of seagulls. Examining the bones helps your child to see how light and how strong they are.

5 & UP

SKILLS

✓ Asking questions

✓ Observation

✓ Making comparisons

Chicken Soup

SKILLS

✓ Asking questions

✓ Observation

✓ Making comparisons

One way to observe bird bones is to make chicken soup. After you've taken the meat off the bones and eaten the soup, tackle those bones again. Pick them as clean as you can and let them dry overnight. The next day, lay them on a tray or two and ask your child to sort them according to weight. Then look at the light bones and see if they're mostly or completely hollow. How are the heavier ones different? Comparing a chicken bone with a beef bone would certainly point out a big difference between a bird and a cow!

Toothless Birds

Another reason why birds are so light is that they have no teeth. Teeth are heavy, so nature dispenses with them for birds. But how do they chew? They've got gizzards that are used to grind up seeds and other food for digestion. Buy some gizzards to examine and maybe cook. Do an experiment to replicate how a gizzard works. Get some seeds that some birds eat and put them in a strong container. Then get a few stones and grind up the seeds with the stones to see how the seeds break down. This is how the gizzard works and also why some birds swallow grit and small pebbles to help this organ work the best.

SKILLS

✓ Asking questions

✓ Observation

✓ Experimenting

✓ Drawing conclusions

Egg Observation

You can't learn about birds without noticing eggs and, of course, nests. Look in books for pictures of the largest egg (the ostrich) and the smallest (the hummingbird). Many eggs are colored so that they fade into their environment for protection. If an egg is fertilized, an embryo lives inside it for about 3 weeks. Unfertilized eggs are the ones we eat. To see the components of an egg, break one (from a chicken) on a dark surface. Even though the shell is hard, it still allows oxygen to penetrate. The yolk is the food supply for the embryo, and the stringy things are what hold the yolk in place. The tiny red dot is the cell that would become an embryo if the egg was fertilized.

Asking Birders

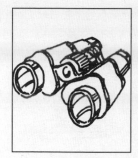

There's nothing like going birding, especially in the spring. If you want to observe specific birds, it's necessary to do some research about birds in your area. Finding a "birder" could be the answer to everything. Call the Audubon Society for your local branch or for other groups that birdwatch. If you live in the city, natural history museums have birding groups, and, of course, if you're in the country there are plenty of birders. Make friends with one and ask about bird sightings. From this list, choose one or two with your child and read up on them in a children's bird book, and then go out and find them. Or you could do it the other way around: find some birds, remember their characteristics, and then look them up. Sometimes all you might see are some feathers, or a nest. If you're looking for an owl, you might find owl pellets underneath its perch. These are the regurgitated fur and bones of all the mice and other rodents owls eat. But maybe a birder could help you find an owl!

5 & UP

SKILLS

✓ Asking questions

✓ Observation

SKILL

✓ Observation

For the Birds

If you're interested in attracting birds, it's a good idea to feed them. There are all kinds of feeders available in stores for different types of birds. You can also spread food on the ground, but then you might end up with a rodent problem. For birds that eat seeds and nuts (those that have short beaks) feed them raw oats, popcorn, barley, bread crumbs, pumpkin seeds, sunflower seeds, or peanuts in a bird feeder. Birds with pointed beaks eat insects. You can buy mealworms at a pet store, or, of course, collect your own worms. In winter, feeding them suet is a good idea. Take a net bag that oranges come in and cut it into a small size. Fill it with suet and hang it with string from a tree. You can buy suet in most supermarkets. Don't forget a water source, both for drinking and bathing. A shallow dish of some sort, placed in a shady, out-of-the-way location is ideal.

Preserving Leaves 1

One way to preserve leaves is a simple tried-and-true method. Lay the leaves without overlapping between sheets of newspaper, put some heavy books on top, and wait. It can take a few days or a few weeks, depending on how much moisture there is in the leaves. If the leaves are very wet you can place them between paper towels first and then wrap in newspaper. If you've collected a lot of leaves, you can pile many sheets of newspaper in layers and press them down with some books.

SKILLS

✓ **Collecting and recording data**

✓ **Observation**

Preserving Leaves 2

SKILLS

✓ **Collecting and recording data**

✓ **Observation**

You can also preserve leaves by heating up an iron on its permanent press setting. Cover a table with newspaper. Get a piece of cardboard and some sheets of waxed paper. Put one piece of waxed paper on top of the piece of cardboard, put a leaf on the waxed paper, cover with another sheet and cover the whole thing with a cloth. Press the iron all over it for one minute. When the leaf cools off, you can either peel off the waxed paper or cut around edges of the leaf and leave the waxed paper attached.

Mix It Up!

Primary colors are red, blue, and yellow. All other colors are secondary ones and are made from mixing primary colors together. Talk about this with your child and then help her put drops of food coloring in medium-size containers of water to make the primary colors. Now put out a lot of other small containers— small glass bottles and jars are the best. Ask your child to use an eye dropper to mix various combinations of the red, blue, and yellow together in the small jars. You might want a container of clear water to rinse the eyedropper occasionally. One of the observations your child will make is that some colors are different shades of one color. Talk about these gradations of color and use the terms "lighter than" and "darker than."

SKILLS

✓ **Asking questions**

✓ **Observation**

✓ **Making a hypothesis**

✓ **Experimenting**

✓ **Drawing conclusions**

323

Putting Out Fires

5 & UP

SKILLS

✓ **Asking questions**

✓ **Observation**

✓ **Drawing conclusions**

An important water source in the neighborhood is the fire hydrant. Where does the water inside the hydrant come from? Is water that is used for putting out fires the same as your drinking water? This is a perfect opportunity to make an appointment to visit your local fire department. There you can ask not only about the hydrants, but also about the pumps and hoses on the fire trucks. How are these filled with water? Of course, if you live in the country, fire hydrants don't exist. Then where do the fire engines get their water from? In this case you'll need to contact a local volunteer fire person for information. Fire trucks alone are pretty fascinating vehicles, so visiting one with an expert on board will provide a valuable learning experience in itself.

Electricity

Following the electricity sources in your house is as interesting as examining the pipes. However, electricity always involves a caution. Make sure you explain the potential dangers of sticking things into outlets, or combining water and electricity. But the idea here is to explore the wiring both inside and outside of your house, not to physically manipulate it. Explain to your child how the big wires outside bring the electricity inside. Go out and look at the poles and the wires and notice how they branch off into different buildings. Then look at the wires in your house and see how many objects are attached to electric wires. Go down to the basement and find the fuse box or circuit breakers, and if possible, do a demonstration of what happens when a particular fuse or circuit breaker shuts off the power. Also, point out the electric meter and explain how the numbers work to measure how much current you use. This would be a good opportunity to talk about saving energy (and money) by using less electricity in your house.

SKILLS

✓ Asking questions

✓ Observation

✓ Making a hypothesis

✓ Experimenting

✓ Drawing conclusions

SKILLS

✓ **Experimenting**

✓ **Drawing conclusions**

Smelling Test

Collect some yogurt containers and wash them well. Into each put some familiar foods, such as cheese, chocolate chips, a cut-up apple or banana, or tuna fish. Cover the top of each container with cloth you can't see through (cheesecloth is good) and put a rubber band around it. Then sniff away. How many of the foods can you identify? Another option is to use nonedible substances such as bits of grass, or soil, or soap, or dog biscuits. Try this on various members of the family and see how well smell alone works for everyone. This could be a good activity for a birthday party.

Macie's Cookies

C ooking is a science, math, and reading activity, but this particular recipe also involves a lot of small motor dexterity because it uses a cookie press. It takes a bit of practice to get the twisting just right to squeeze out the perfect-size cookie. Cookie presses come with various design inserts to produce all shapes of cookies, but if you twist too much the cookie will be fat and lose its design.

SKILLS

✓ Observation

✓ Measurement

✓ Small motor skills

    Cream 1 lb of sweet butter with 1½ cups sugar and 1 tsp. of salt and 1 tsp. of baking powder. Sift 5 cups of flour. Beat 2 eggs. Add the eggs to the sugar mixture with 1 tsp. of vanilla. Now gradually incorporate the flour into the mixture. Cool the dough in the refrigerator for 1 hour, and then take out only enough to fit in the cookie press. Twist your shapes onto a cookie sheet, and decorate with candied cherries, sprinkles, or chocolate chips. Bake 10 minutes in a 400 degree oven.

Cooking a Pumpkin

This recipe is definitely a scientific discovery! In the fall, when pumpkins are plentiful, plan with your child to make some pumpkin bread or cookies. But instead of cutting up the pumpkin and boiling it in a pot, do it this way. Preheat the oven to 350 degrees. Place the whole pumpkin on a cookie sheet and bake it until it collapses. It would be very dramatic if you had a glass oven door to watch the changes, but it will still be a fascinating experience to see it when it's cooked! When it's cooled, your child can cut it apart with your help and pull out the seeds. Peel it, and you've got the makings of any pumpkin recipe.

Fruit Salad

A perfect recipe for young children to make is fruit salad. Go to the store with your child and select some fruit for the salad. Bring it home and make sure you wash it well with her help. Even melons these days should be washed before you cut them. Explain to your child that there are germs that need to be washed off food before you eat it. If your child is quite young, make sure you select enough fruit that is soft so that the cutting up is easy for him. You start by cutting an apple in half, and then your child can cut it into smaller pieces. Give him a tray so the whole process is contained. Also very useful are plastic serrated knives—they'll cut in a back-and-forth motion and they're safe. Just make sure that you give your child small enough pieces to cut by himself and don't do much cutting yourself. You'll be surprised how diligent he'll be at this task!

SKILLS

✓ Observation
✓ Manual dexterity

329

SKILLS

✓ Experimenting

✓ Drawing
conclusions

Tasting Test

To develop a finer sense of taste, blindfold your child and have her guess what food she's eating. You can choose all kinds of foods, but make sure there's a range of strong flavors and subtle ones. If your family is into garlic, maybe a small piece of that might be a choice or perhaps a caper from that fish recipe you use. In any case, don't neglect a bit of sugar, or salt, or even chocolate. Does not being able to see the food affect how well you can taste it? Ask your child to hold her nose and try the same foods after removing the blindfold. Is it easier to identify the tastes without seeing the food or without smelling it?

Physical Development Activities

Children develop as whole individuals, integrating their senses, their minds, and their bodies in everything they do. Physical development in young children is hard to miss, and being able to master physical tasks and to use their bodies as a resource is critical to building a sense of competency. Being successful in activities that foster both small motor skills and large motor skills is as necessary for a young child as developing social skills or acquiring language.

Some of the activities in this section are based on eye/hand coordination learning experiences created by Maria Montessori. Montessori understood that children naturally seek order in their world and that activities that appeal to both their minds and their senses are particularly valuable. Modeling adults and using adult materials are also important steps in a child's development. Although mastering basic eye/hand coordination takes time, children derive much satisfaction from repeating things; and as they do, both their concentration and their confidence grow.

Sewing

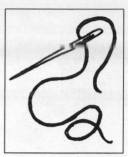

Children love to sew, but it helps to have the right materials. Although some can manage a blanket stitch or a hem stitch after help getting started, using mesh from a crafts store might make it even easier. Bear in mind that young children will need you around most of the time while they sew, the type of eye/hand coordination required is hard for them.

Cut a piece of mesh about 3 in. by 3 in. Thread a large metal needle or a plastic one with yarn. Double-knot the yarn and demonstrate to your child that you "go up from the bottom" and "down from the top" with the needle. If you think your child is up to it, ask him what kind of design or pattern he might like to make. A pattern of alternating colors could be appealing. An older child could trace his initials with a marker and sew them. Then he could fill in the background with a different color.

5 & UP

SKILLS

✓ **Eye/hand coordination**

✓ **Imaginative thinking**

✓ **Patterns**

A Fixer-Upper

SKILLS

✓ Small motor skills

✓ Patterns

✓ Imaginative thinking

✓ Drawing and painting

This creative activity also helps develop small motor skills. Find a piece of wooden furniture that looks pretty worn-out and help your child paint it. Not just an ordinary paint job, but one that has her own design on it. Suppose it's a chair or a small chest. Discuss with her the different colors it could be. It would really help if you saw a piece of hand-painted furniture somewhere, like those small chairs from Mexico. But talk about different designs. Maybe each leg could be a different color and the back and seat different colors as well. And what about patterns or pictures after the undercoat is dry? If she wants it to be her own piece of furniture, she might want her name on it and maybe a picture of her cat. Or it could be a "word" chair, with words printed all over the place. The possibilities are endless! Make sure to help her get the undercoat on fairly evenly. Use the finished piece as part of your home furnishings.

Collage a Tray

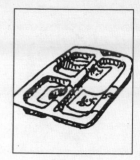

This activity is both artistic and functional. Get some sort of paper tray such as the kind of paper plate that is divided into sections. You can use this to make a very attractive tray in which you can put keys, change, and other small items on the hall table, or jewelry in the bedroom. Ask your child to cut out colorful pictures from magazines. Make sure none of them are too large, so there will be a variety of them on the tray. Then help your child glue them to the tray, making sure that they are pressed down in all the corners of the compartments. To make sure the whole plate is covered, small strips and pieces of magazine pictures might need to be cut and glued onto the edges—a patchwork effect only makes it look better. For best results, do the underside, too. When it's dry you (not your child) should shellac it all over to make it durable and give it extra gloss.

5 & UP

SKILLS

✓ **Manual dexterity**

✓ **Imaginative thinking**

333

Hit the Stick

SKILLS

✓ Eye/hand
coordination

Here's a game for two people to play with a ball that develops eye/hand coordination. It's probably best played on a driveway or other flat surface outside. Find a stick that's not too big and put it in a space in the middle of the two players. Mark this space with a chalkmark or a rock. How far the players stand from the stick depends on who's playing—the farther away, the more coordination is required. The object is to hit the stick and move it when you bounce the ball to the other person. You can be concrete about this and make a mark with chalk next to the stick each time it's moved, or you can be more laid-back and just try to move the stick without keeping score. The player who moves the stick the most is the winner.

Junk Sculpture

When you have young children around, it's a good idea to save things. Not forever, but stuff that can be recycled into activities for children. Keep all kinds of cardboard, such as tubes, dividers, small boxes, or tiny boxes. Also keep all kinds of plastic; containers of every size, "popcorn" bubbles from packages, plastic insertions from new shirts, and the like. Save paper, pieces of cloth, odd bits of cellophane, orange juice containers, styrofoam pieces. If you have an ongoing supply of such riches in a corner of your house, you'll always have something for children to do. Junk sculpture involves many skills that strengthen your child's small motor development. Putting things together so that they make a balanced arrangement is tricky business, and it takes mathematical thinking about balance and proportion to make it work. Be a background helper in this, but let your child conjure up how he wants it to look.

SKILLS

✓ Eye/hand coordination

✓ Imaginative thinking

335

Scooping Pebbles

SKILLS

✓ Eye/hand
  coordination

✓ Manual dexterity

This activity will help young children improve manual dexterity and also provide them with a satisfying tactile experience. Get two small bowls, a small scoop, and a collection of small pebbles or those smooth polished stones you find in gardening stores. You could also use beans. Fill one bowl with the stones and ask your child to practice using the scoop to transfer them to the second bowl. Seems simple, but to a young child learning to master fine motor skills it's challenging and satisfying. Your child will notice the sound the stones make when they're scooped, how smooth they are, and their coolness to the touch.

Scooping Balls

This activity for a young child helps develop eye/hand coordination. Get two medium-size bowls, some scoops of different sizes, and four or five ping-pong balls. The object of this exercise is to transfer 1 ball at a time with the scoop from one bowl to the other. Depending on the size of the scoop, or your child's inclination, she might want to use two hands for this at first—one to hold the scoop and one to push the ball into it. This is a fine way to start, but the goal is to scoop these balls up single-handedly. For a young child, scooping the ball up then balancing it on the scoop to reach the other bowl can be difficult at first, but with practice, she can be successful.

3 & UP

SKILLS

✓ Eye/hand coordination

Ladling Water

SKILLS

✓ Eye/hand
coordination

This activity helps your child master small motor skills by working with water. Get two medium-size bowls and a soup ladle. Fill one bowl with water and ask your child to ladle the water to the second bowl. It might help to place the bowl on a tray, a towel, or both. You might also change the distance between the bowls for an added challenge. Add primary color food dye to the two bowls for an additional lesson in making colors.

Spooning Escargots

This is a fine motor activity that uses a tiny mustard spoon, marbles, and an escargot dish. Put 6 marbles in a small bowl and ask your child to scoop up 1 at a time with the spoon and transfer the marble to a space in the escargot dish. Then reverse the process by spooning each marble back to the bowl. Placing all the equipment on a tray should help keep the materials organized. A young child's fine motor skills are literally shaky, and such a thing as a tiny spoon is a challenge to manipulate, not to mention using it to pick up a marble. But the delicacy of these materials appeals to young children—just as picking up pebbles on the beach or peering at a colony of ants does.

3 & UP

SKILLS

✓ Eye/hand coordination

339

Tweezing

SKILLS

✓ Eye/hand coordination

To prepare for this activity, help your child learn how to hold and squeeze a tweezer. Practice at first picking up scraps of material, cotton balls, or small wads of paper. When some degree of mastery is achieved, get either an escargot dish or a small paint palette and a small bowl of marbles. Ask your child to transfer 1 marble at a time to the depression in the palette or dish with the tweezer. Tricky stuff, at first, even for an adult, but a worthwhile exercise for developing small motor skills.

Play Modeling Clay

To make play modeling clay, mix together 2 cups of flour, 1 cup of salt, water, and 1 tablespoon of cooking oil. Just the making of the clay is a learning experience. As they participate they can see and feel the changes that take place when certain ingredients are combined. Have your child measure the flour and dump it into a bowl. Then add the salt and oil. Have a measuring cup full of water handy, but don't expect to use it all. The trick is to add the water slowly and mush the stuff around. Little by little, the stuff goes from crumbly to pliable and resembles bread dough. To add color, a few drops of food coloring can be squeezed in. Control over the food color is recommended; there is no mess like the mess too much food color makes!

Play modeling clay is wonderful stuff and is suitable for many engaging activities. Aside from the delight of squeezing it and making "pretend" food or snakes, a good learning activity is to help your child roll it into alphabet letters. Play modeling clay itself is not meant to be kept permanently, although if stored in plastic bag in the refrigerator, it will last a week or two.

SKILLS

✓ **Imaginative thinking**

✓ **Small motor development**

✓ **Manual dexterity**

✓ **Measurement**

SKILLS

✓ **Imaginative thinking**

✓ **Small motor development**

✓ **Manual dexterity**

✓ **Measurement**

Cornstarch Clay

To create a more permanent alphabet, use cornstarch clay instead of play modeling clay. This dries and doesn't crumble and can be painted. Of course, many other items can be made with this recipe, such as holiday ornaments, figurines, and so on.

To make the cornstarch clay, you will need 1 cup of cornstarch, 2 cups of salt, and water (probably $1\frac{1}{3}$ cup or so). Put salt and $\frac{2}{3}$ cup water in a pot and bring to a boil. Mix cornstarch in bowl with rest of water and stir. Blend the two mixes and knead to form a clay shape and mold clay into letters or other shapes, as desired. Air-dry for a few hours. Paint when dry.

Sponging It Up

Use two medium-size bowls for this activity. Put the bowls right next to each other. Fill one no more than halfway with water. For added attraction, you might add a few drops of food color to the water. Get a small sponge—a natural one that fits your child's hand would be perfect—and ask your child to put the sponge in the water, then pick it up and let it stop dripping before transferring it to the empty bowl and squeezing out the water. One variation is to put only the amount of water in the bowl that the sponge will pick up—you would need to experiment first to figure this out. When the second bowl has the water in it, simply reverse the process.

3 & UP

SKILLS

✓ Eye/hand coordination

Nuts and Bolts

SKILLS

✓ Eye/hand
coordination

This activity uses a twisting action. Get some nuts and bolts of different sizes and put them all out on a tray. Then demonstrate how to twist the nut off one bolt and ask your child to remove the rest of the nuts. Then select a bolt and a nut and see if you can twist it on by turning in the opposite direction. If it doesn't fit, continue to try other nuts. Your child will notice that the largest bolt and nut takes the longest time to twist on and off. Mention that the ridges on both the nut and bolt have to fit each other, and also point out how you twist one way to remove the nut and the other way to put it back on.

Stringing Macaroni

Simple stringing activities help to strengthen small motor development. A good one is to string various sizes of macaroni. Use a piece of yarn that you have dipped into melted wax on one end. At the other end tie a noodle in place. Then show your child how to hold one piece of macaroni and push the waxed end of the string through its hole. You might count with her as she goes along. When all the noodles are strung, she can pull them off and start again with different ones. As her dexterity develops, she can use smaller noodles to string.

3 & UP

SKILLS

✓ Eye/hand
   coordination

Spring Cleaning

SKILLS

✓ **Eye/hand coordination**

✓ **Small motor development**

For a young child, washing things can be a very satisfying experience. You could start with a dirty surface such as a table or a small section of floor. (If the surface has a few extra dirty spots, so much the better.) Get together a bucket, a small scrub brush, a towel, a sponge, and an apron for your child to wear. Help him fill the bucket halfway with water and add a few drops of dishwashing detergent. Then ask him to take the brush, dip it into the water, and then to rub the brush on the surface in a circular motion, covering the surface. Then he needs to wet the sponge, squeeze it, and use it to wipe up the suds from the brush. Your child should rinse the sponge from time to time when it gets too soapy. If there are particular spots that still need work, he can use the brush and then sponge again in these places. Not only do such practical jobs matter in giving a young child a sense or responsibility in his environment, but also they provide opportunities to develop basic motor skills.

Shoe Shine

SKILLS

✓ **Eye/hand coordination**

In this world of sneakers, it's hard to believe that there's such a thing as shoe polish, but some shoes still need it. It's a useful activity for your child to learn, and it can help increase manual dexterity. Start by finding a pair of shoes and show your child how you can put your hand into a shoe and hold it in place while it's being polished. Ask her to use a rag or applicator to rub into the can of polish and when that's ready, to stick her hand into the shoe and rub the shoe all over with the polish. When this is done, she should close the polish can and use the buffing brush to shine the shoe in a brisk brushing motion. Don't forget to wash hands when the job is done.

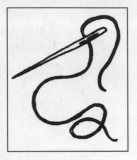

Threading a Needle

SKILLS

✓ Eye/hand
   coordination

✓ Small motor
   development

To help develop eye/hand coordination and fine motor control, an excellent activity is to learn to thread a needle. Get a large blunt end needle from a crafts store and some colored yarn or embroidery thread. One way to do this is to ask your child to loop the end of the yarn over the eye of the needle and to pull the yarn through with his thumb and index finger. Another way is to push the end of the yarn straight through. You can either knot the end of the thread or not, but to practice threading, pull the thread out and try again.

Peeling Carrots

To increase small motor coordination, learning to peel carrots is a good activity. First see that your child washes her hands, an important habit to form when dealing with food. Show her how to hold the carrot with thumb underneath and four fingers on top. With the other hand hold the carrot peeler with her thumb on the inside of the handle and her forefinger on top of blade. Peel away from the body and turn the carrot until it is completely peeled. You might want to cut off the ends of the carrot yourself or guide your child using a serrated knife. Then eat and enjoy!

4 & UP

SKILLS

✓ Eye/hand coordination

✓ Small motor development

Fabric Textures

For an activity dealing with the subtleties of textures, find some swatches of fabrics of different texture, but make sure you have two of each kind. You can do this activity with eyes open or closed, but the point is to observe and compare the different types of fabric and then to match them. Suppose you have some satin, velvet, heavy tapestry, or corduroy. Ask your child to feel them all over and describe how they feel. To make it harder, ask her to close her eyes and put out six swatches. Then ask her to place together any that feel the same. Afterward, have her open her eyes and check her work.

Crayon Grating

An interesting art activity that also teaches how to use a grater is crayon grating. Gather together some crayons (big ones are best), and remove the wrappers. Then holding the grater over a bowl, demonstrate how to rub the crayon up and down the grater. Use different color crayons, and have about a cupful when you're done. Sprinkle some on a piece of waxed paper, cover with another sheet, and rub over with an iron on "warm." After the melted wax has cooled, you or your child can cut around the edges of the melted crayons. Then make a hole in the top, put some yarn through it, and hang the decoration on the window.

4 & UP

SKILLS

✓ **Eye/hand coordination**

✓ **Small motor development**

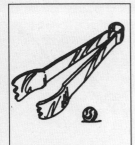

SKILLS

✓ Eye/hand
  coordination

✓ Small motor
  development

Marble Painting

For a printing activity that also uses small motor dexterity, place a marble in a small dish of paint. Put a sheet of paper on a tray. Then, with a pair of tongs, your child can grasp the marble (no mean feat), place it on the paper and then roll it around the paper and tray to make a design. You could have a few marbles, each in different colors of paint and use the tongs to pick each one up one at a time to liven up the design.

Straw Painting

A fun activity to do with your child is straw painting on paper. First, mix some poster paint with a little water so it isn't so thick and pour some of it into the middle of a piece of paper. Then show your child how to hold a straw an inch or so above the paper and blow through it to direct the paint on the paper. You could put dabs of different colored paint at spots on the paper so your child can create a particularly colorful design.

SKILLS

✓ Eye/hand coordination

✓ Imaginative thinking

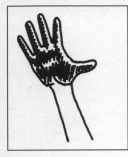

Finger Painting

SKILLS

✓ Small motor development

✓ Eye/hand coordination

✓ Imaginative thinking

Using your fingers to make designs certainly enhances small motor dexterity, but if you use finger paint, you've got a wonderful sensory experience as well. Why not make your own? Beat together ½ cup of instant cold water starch, ½ cup of soap flakes (not powder), and 5 oz. of water. Add some food coloring and mix it up. You could buy special finger paint paper or you could choose a Formica surface (like a child's table) to paint on. Just use your hand to scoop some of the paint out onto the surface and let your child go! Part of the experience is, at least at first, to revel in the feel of it all, but eventually your child might very well want to use her finger to write her name or draw. If you use a surface to paint on, cleaning up can also be a valuable part of the activity. Have a bucket of water and sponge handy, and demonstrate how to squeeze the sponge and then use it to wipe the surface many times.

Pincushions

Whether or not your child has practiced threading a needle, she still might like making a pincushion with your help. You can use all kinds of things for stuffing. Old pantyhose is perfect, but you can also buy a bag of stuffing from a crafts store. If the pincushion is a success, maybe a pillow will follow. Your child should choose some fabric she likes, maybe from some outgrown clothing. Then show her how to do a simple hem stitch or possibly a blanket stitch. You might also find that she'll do both, as blanket stitches tend to show up automatically in young children's sewing. The challenge is to use just one or the other, but of course, a combination has a nice spontaneous look to it.

5 & UP

SKILLS

✓ Eye/hand coordination

355

Pressing Flowers

SKILLS

✓ Small motor development

✓ Imaginative thinking

Doing a flower pressing activity will teach your child a lot about the composition of flowers. For example, flowers have a lot of moisture inside them, and also different flowers and leaves change their color after they're dried. This is something you will learn with experience, and if you decide to frame any of your flowers or to make bookmarks, you'll learn which plants are most pleasing when dried. You'll need a lot of newspaper for pressing, and some heavy objects like books to use as weights. Also it's best if the flowers can be as flat as possible when you lay them on the paper. This might involve cutting away some of the thicker parts of them. When you've chosen your flowers, line them up on newspaper so that they're not touching. Then cover with more newspaper and put heavy books all over the surface of the paper. Leave them for 1 week or so and check on them. The real professionals use blotting paper first, then newspaper and leave them for a month, sometimes changing the newspaper only. So you decide how professional you want to be.

Pressed Flower Pictures

To mount pressed flowers for framing, get some poster board of a complementary color for your flowers and cut it to fit a frame. Then try different arrangements on the poster board. You can always cut some flowers and leaves apart and use them as part of the picture. For example, you might make a border of leaves around the center arrangement, or you could sprinkle the background with rose petals. Just make sure the flowers will be pressed tightly into the frame when you're done. To glue them on the poster board, use a small brush or even a toothpick. You can also make bookmarks with your child from pressed flowers. Simply cut strips of poster board, arrange the flowers into a design, glue them and cover the entire bookmark (front and back) with clear contact paper.

4 & UP

SKILLS

✓ Imaginative thinking

✓ Eye/hand coordination

Potato Prints

Your child can make many beautiful prints using ordinary things around the house. Some of these ordinary things are foods, but some can also be leaves, corks, feathers, or even large buttons. You can also paint details on the prints themselves once they're on paper or paint the background of each print.

Using a potato as a stencil is a popular way to print. After washing and peeling the potato, cut it into halves or quarters. Then you have two choices: you can either help your child cut out a relief design in one piece of potato; or you can cut the potato into pieces and shapes that you will use as the stencils. Obviously, cutting a design in relief is harder, so the design should be simple—maybe a circle or a triangle. Another thing to remember is that potatoes need to be recycled daily as they get soft quickly.

Get out some paper or pieces of smooth fabric and pour some poster paint into saucers and dip the stencil. Each stencil should have its own color. Then print away!

Vegetable Prints

P rinting with other vegetables is also
fun. Instead of cutting out relief
stencils, many vegetables can simply be
cut in half and printed as is. For example,
a pepper cut in half and dipped in paint
can make a very attractive print. You can
also use all kinds of objects from outside,
such as pine cones, leaves, or twigs. Stick
a piece of tape that you've first wrapped
around your finger on the back of each
object. Otherwise, these objects can be
hard to pick up as you transfer them from
paint to paper. To make any print, make
sure you experiment with the amount of
paint to apply on any object. Sometimes,
the third or fourth printing is the one you
like best. You can either dip the object
into a saucer of poster paint or you can
brush paint onto the surface.

SKILLS

✓ **Eye/hand
coordination**

✓ **Imaginative
thinking**

Shell Out!

SKILLS

✓ Small motor development

✓ Eye/hand coordination

✓ Imaginative thinking

If you've collected shells with your child through the years, you and he can make some attractive items that definitely require small motor dexterity. If you have some small gift boxes handy, designing a shell arrangement to cover the box is a fun activity. Your child might want to paint the box first, inside and out. For a younger child, just making a spontaneous arrangement on the cover, or even all over the sides is a good idea. If your child is older, he might want to make a drawing of the design first so he can follow it as he glues the shells in place. These boxes could make wonderful personalized gifts for friends and relatives.

Quilting

Quilts can be made out of paper or fabric and can be both a math and reading activity. Making a pattern with the squares and fitting them together is math, but the quilt could have a theme relating to literature. Suppose your child thinks of some favorite books, and you help her write their names on separate squares that she could decorate with pictures of the characters. If these pieces are paper, they can be glued onto a backing, such as part of an old sheet, or a large paper. They also could be fabric squares and the writing and pictures can be done in fabric markers. These squares can then be sewn together with a large needle and embroidery thread. You could use light-colored pieces of felt for the material as these are easier to sew together.

SKILLS

✓ **Eye/hand coordination**

✓ **Patterns**

✓ **Drawing and painting**

Paper Mosaic

SKILLS

✓ **Small motor development**

✓ **Imaginative thinking**

Making a mosaic picture with lots of small squares of paper is a challenge. Help your child cut out strips of different colored paper and then further cut the strips into squares. It would be helpful if you could find some examples of mosaic art to share with your child—not that she should try for such sophisticated work, but to see how the small pieces fit together. Sometimes mosaics can just be designs and this could be the place for your child to begin. Glue the squares in lines, not haphazardly. You can also design a simple shape of an animal or flower. Help guide your child to think of using different colors for the petals or the features of the animal, but remember, her ideas count more.

Toss It Around

This homemade game surely helps develop manual dexterity! Glue the bottoms of two paper cups together. When the cups are dry, your child can collage them with magazine pictures or decorate them with markers. Then use the cups to toss something like a small ball or marble from the top cup and catch it in the bottom one. This could be played with other people and your child can set the timer and see how many times each person can make a catch in one minute.

5 & UP

SKILLS

✓ **Large and small motor development**

✓ **Eye/hand coordination**

✓ **Imaginative thinking**

363

Rhythm Band

SKILLS

✓ Large and small motor development

✓ Eye/hand coordination

✓ Imaginative thinking

There's nothing like having your own rhythm band, especially if your child makes all the instruments. There's a large variety to choose from, but you could choose them all and invite all the children on the block to have a concert. Coffee cans should have both ends removed and then be covered with plastic lids. For drumsticks, use chopsticks, wooden spoons, or hands. Tone blocks are simply small blocks of wood with sandpaper glued to them. These are rubbed together for sound. Rattles can be any kind of small container filled with pebbles, rice, or beans. Two pot lids make excellent cymbals. Bell bracelets can be made by sewing small bells to wrist bands of elastic. A kazoo can be made from a paper towel tube in which a few holes are cut. Put a piece of waxed paper at one end with an elastic band and your child can hum into the other end while covering and uncovering the holes with her fingers. And don't forget the grass whistle. Find a wide piece of grass, have your child press it between her thumbs, press her thumbs against her lips and blow!

Gymnastics

All kinds of exercise are wonderful large muscle builders. Children like to do "real" exercises, especially if they're joined by a few others. How about pushups, or stretching high in the air, or touching toes, or twisting, or jogging around the yard? You could also set up an obstacle course in your yard, and ask the children to use various movements, such as skipping, or flapping like birds, to go around the obstacles. Pretending to be animals is also good exercise—slithering like a snake, jumping like a kangaroo, galloping like a horse, slinking like a cat. Children's bodies need to grow and develop, that's why children are so physical and sometimes a little structured exercise can be fun as well.

4 & UP

SKILLS

✓ Large motor development

✓ Imaginative thinking

Resources

Catalogs can be ordered from the following companies that provide many materials for schools. You can order books and reading materials that are often used in reading instruction in schools from:

The Wright Group
19201 120th Avenue, N.E.
Bothell, WA 98011
800-648-2970

Math manipulatives and books, as well as materials for science and language arts, can be ordered from:

Cuisenaire
Dale Seymour Publications
P.O. Box 5026
White Plains, NY 10602-5026
800-237-0338

All kinds of learning materials for language, math, and science activities can be ordered from:

Lakeshore Learning Materials
2695 E. Dominguez Street
P.O. Box 6261
Carson, CA 90749
800-421-5354

You can order science equipment and materials, including live insects, foods for the insects, terrariums, and vivariums, from:

Carolina Biological Supply Company
2700 York Road
Burlington, NC 27215
800-334-5551

Index (By age level)

369

5 & UP

371

6 & UP

MARY WEAVER has been a teacher of early childhood education in New York City for over twenty-five years. For the past fifteen years, she has taught K-1 (Kindergarten/First Grade) in Manhattan in the public school system and before that in private schools. She is actively involved with the Bank Street School of Education as a support teacher for interns in their Early Childhood graduate program.